WONDERDADS

THE BEST DAD/CHILD ACTIVITIES IN THE TRIANGLE

CONTACT WONDERDADS

WonderDads books may be purchased for educational and promotional use. For information, please email us at store@wonderdads.com.

If you are interested in partnership opportunities with WonderDads, please email us at partner@wonderdads.com.

If you are interested in selling WonderDads books and other products in your region, please email us at hiring@wonderdads.com.

For corrections, recommendations on what to include in future versions of the book, updates or any other information, please email us at info@wonderdads.com.

©2011 WonderDads, Inc.

Book Authored by Stephen Raburn & the WonderDads Staff

Cover and book design by Crystal Langley. Layout by Angela Bullin & the WonderDads Staff.

All rights reserved. Printed in the United States of America.

ISBN: 978-1-935153-52-8

First Printing, 2011

10 9 8 7 6 5 4 3 2 1

WONDERDADS
THE TRIANGLE
Table of Contents

WELCOME TO WONDERDADS THE TRIANGLE

Like so many other Dads, I love being with my kids, but struggle to find the right work/home balance. We are a part of a generation where Dads play much more of an active role with their kids, yet the professional and financial strains are greater than ever. We hope that the ideas in this book make it a little easier to be inspired to do something that makes you a hero in the eyes of your children.

This part of our children's lives goes by too fast, but the memories from a WonderDads inspired trip, event, meal, or activity last a long time (and will probably be laughed about when they grow up). So plan a Daddy day once a week, make breakfast together every Saturday morning, watch your football team every Sunday, or whatever works for you, and be amazed how long they will remember the memories and how good you will feel about yourself in the process.

Our warmest welcome to WonderDads.

Sincerely,

Jonathan Aspatore, **Founder & Dad**
Charlie (4) and Luke (3)

THE TOP 10 OVERALL BEST DAD/CHILD THINGS TO DO

THE BEST OF THE TRIANGLE

THE TOP 5 DAD/CHILD ACTIVITIES

THE TOP 5 DAD/CHILD OUTDOOR PARKS AND RECREATION

THE TOP 5 DAD/CHILD THINGS TO DO ON A RAINY DAY

THE TOP 5 DAD/CHILD THINGS TO DO ON A HOT DAY

THE TOP 5 DAD/CHILD FULL-DAY ACTIVITIES

THE TOP 5 DAD/CHILD SPLURGES 💲💲💲

THE TOP 5 DAD/CHILD MOST MEMORABLE

THE BEST DAD/CHILD
RESTAURANTS

ANNA'S PIZZERIA

Apex

100 Salem St.
Apex, NC 27502
(919) 267-6237 | www.annaspizzeria.com
Calzones, paninis, wraps, pasta, and pizza. Kid's meals are hearty and inexpensive.

HIBACHI XPRESS

Apex

2021 Creekside Landing
Apex, NC 27502
(919) 290-1008 | www.hibachixpress.com
Kid's menu includes chicken, steak, shrimp, tempura served with rice or noodles and a drink ranging in price from $2.75 to $3.50. Now, that's a deal. Dad prices are reasonable, as well.

SPARKS WINGS AND RIBS

Apex

5490 Apex Pky.
Apex, NC 27502
(919) 303-0074 | www.sparkswingsandribs.com
Not the kind of place to bring the kids in their good clothes. Messy but delectable ribs and award-winning burgers. Magic and laughter with Happy Dan the Magic Man equals a meal plus fun, magic and balloons. Kids also eat free from 6-8 pm. Call to confirm Happy Dan days.

CARRBURRITOS

Carrboro

711 Rosemary St.
Carrboro, NC 27510
(919) 933-8226 | www.carrburritos.com
Extra points for such a creative name. Locals consistently vote Carrburritos THE best Mexican restaurant in town; always fresh ingredients and great vegan options (this is Carrboro, after all).

MAPLE VIEW ICE CREAM PARLOR

Carrboro

100 East Weaver St.
Carrboro, NC 27510.
(919) 967-6842 | www.mapleviewfarm.com/locations/carrboro.php
Go to Weaver Street Market in downtown Carrboro, look for the cow awning across the street: you just found Maple View Ice Cream Parlor. Enjoy scrumptious homemade ice cream from the nearby dairy farm on the swings out front or walk back across the street and sit out under a shade tree. On a nice day you'll be joined by droves of locals... students on their laptops, kids climbing trees, perhaps an impromptu string quartet. This is truly one of the reasons we live in the Triangle.

PLANET SMOOTHIE

Carrboro

1939 High House Rd.
Cary, NC 27519
(919) 656-0228 | www.planetsmoothie.com
Kids will enjoy delicious smoothies like the Purple Primate or the Peanut Butter Dream while dad has his organic, energy-packed Berry Bada-Bing.

BAVARIAN BRATHAUS OF CARY

Cary

6464 Tryon Rd.
Cary, NC 27518
(919) 859-5299 | www.carysbrats.blogspot.com
Transport your kids to Germany without getting on a plane. The kid's menu could be called "brats for brats."

BLUE MOON BAKERY

Cary

115 W. Chatham St.
Cary, NC 27511
(919) 319-6654 | www.bluemoonbakery.com
If you find yourself in downtown Cary craving a cupcake, this is the place for you! Cakes, pies, breads, breakfast.... Yum.

CIRCUS FAMILY

Cary

611 E. Chatham St.
Cary, NC 27511
(919) 467-1220
Kid-friendly, cash-only and no frills. Grab a milk shake, hotdog or hamburger at this classic roadside family fast food joint.

DANNY'S BAR-B-QUE

Cary

311 Ashville Ave.
Cary, NC 27511
(919) 851-5541 | www.dannysbarbque.com
Tasty barbeque and more (catfish, charbroiled hamburgers); "piglets" menu (under 10) is reasonably priced with generous portions.

FIVE GUYS

Cary

1856 Boulderstone Way
Cary, NC 27519
(919) 465-1936 | www.fiveguys.com
Burgers and fries in a bright, fast and friendly place. Inexpensive, with good vegetarian options, as well.

RESTAURANTS

15

RESTAURANTS

HENRY'S GELATO
Cary

1063 Darrington Dr.
Cary, NC 27513
(919) 358-5888 | www.henrysgelato.com
24 wonderful gelato flavors to choose from. Kids love gelato. Other locations in North Hills Shopping Center and Lafayette Village.

LOOP PIZZA GRILL
Cary

1207 Kildare Farm Rd.
Cary, NC 27511
(919) 657-0330 | www.looppizzagrill.com
Chicago-style deep dish pizza, fab burgers... try the hand-dipped Oreo milkshake.

MICHELANGELO'S PIZZA
Cary

941 N. Harrison
Cary, NC 27513
(919) 467-0013 | michelangelospizza.com
Here's a deal for you: the all-you-can-eat buffet includes pizza, the pasta of the day, ziti, spaghetti and meatballs, lasagna, shells, elbows, salad and dessert pizzas... all for just $2.99 for kids under ten (lunch or dinner). A little more for dads, but still a great deal if your family can put away a pizza or two.

TANGERINE CAFE
Cary

2422 SW Cary Pky
Cary, NC 27513
(919) 468-8688 | www.tangerinecafecary.com
Fresh, flavorful Asian cuisine in a cool, casual atmosphere. Ask about their charitable giving program they call "You eat, we give."

Z PIZZA
Cary

96 Cornerstone Dr.
Cary, NC 27519
(919) 465-9009 | www.zpizza.com
Z pizzas are made with organic wheat flour prepared fresh every day, hand-thrown and fire-baked. Toppings include organic tomato sauce and MSG-free pepperoni. Gourmet salads and sandwiches are also on the menu. Two other locations in Raleigh. Because if you're going to eat pizza twice a week, it ought to be good for you, right?

BRIXX
Chapel Hill

501 Meadowmont Village Cir.
Chapel Hill, NC 27517
(919) 968-4224 | www.brixxpizza.com
Brick-oven pizza in a casual, kid-friendly environment makes this pizza joint one of our favorites.

CAROLINA CONFECTIONARY COMPANY
Chapel Hill

11624-A Hwy 15-501
Chapel Hill, 27517
(919) 967-7500 | carolinaconfectionarycompany.com
Serving toffee from a recipe handed down through the generations, French and Belgian style truffles and other fine chocolates, this is a special sweet treat.

CREPES-VERONIQUE
Chapel Hill

431 W. Franklin St.
Chapel Hill, NC 27616
(919) 928-6768 | crepes-veronique.com
Hot, fragrant crepes made before your eyes. The savory breakfast crepes are packed with eggs and fresh ingredients like cheese, ham and mushrooms. Or just go straight for the sweet stuff; chocolate and coconut, apple caramel and other tasty treats your kids will find worthy of finishing their veggies for.

FLYING BURRITO
Chapel Hill

746 MLK, Jr. Blvd.
Chapel Hill, NC 27514
(919) 967-7744 | www.originalflyingburrito.com
Southwestern flare with a Carolina accent. $2 taco menu is a suitable substitute for a kid's menu.

I LOVE NY PIZZA
Chapel Hill

106 W. Franklin St.
Chapel Hill, NC 27516
(919) 968-4224
A great place to pop in for a slice of thin-crust pizza before or after a Tar Heel game.

LICKITY SPLIT ICE CREAM
Chapel Hill

503 Meadowmont Village Cir.
Chapel Hill, NC 27517
(919) 929-8402
Hot dogs + hand-dipped ice cream = happy kids.

TANDOOR INDIAN RESTAURANT
Chapel Hill

1301 E. Franklin St.
Chapel Hill, NC 27514
(919) 967-6622 | www.tandoorindian.com
Fun, festive atmosphere, authentic Indian cuisine when your kid's taste buds are ready to experience the explosion which is curry, chutney, masala and somosas.

17

AMELIA'S
Durham

905 W. Main St.
Durham, NC 27701
(919) 683-5600

Brightleaf Square café which is connected to Chamas Brazilian Steak-house, offering pastries, desserts, chocolates, gourmet coffees, soups and sandwiches and delicious gelato. Tip: Amelia's just happens to be right in front of the stage in the courtyard at Brightleaf Square, so their outdoor seating is front-row seating during the summer concert series.

BEN AND JERRY'S
Durham

609 Broad St.
Durham, NC 27705
(919) 416-6128 | www.benandjerrys.com

Menu totals over 50 ice cream, frozen yogurt and sorbet products. Open 7 days a week, Noon to 10 pm during the week. Open until 11 pm on Fridays and Saturdays. It's never too early to introduce your kid to Cherry Garcia!

BEYU CAFFE
Durham

335 W. Main St.
Durham, NC 27701
www.beyucaffe.com

One of the gems of Durham's downtown renaissance. Great atmosphere, great food, great live music, including renowned local and national acts. After the kid's bellies are full, have them sprawl out on one of the comfy sofas in front of the stage and be lulled to lala land with some fine smooth jazz.

BISCUITVILLE
Durham

1129 W. Club Blvd. at I-85
Durham, NC 27701
(919) 286-4373 | www.biscuitville.com

Fresh biscuits and southern breakfast fare. Opens at 5:30 which makes it a good first stop for breakfast on those long, got-to-get-an-early-start road trips to Grandma's house.

BLUE COFFEE
Durham

202 Corcoron St.
Durham, NC 27701
(919) 683-5282 | www.bluecoffeecafe.net

Great place to grab a hot dog or veggie burger and bag of chips, topped off with an ice cream cone when you're downtown with the kids. Comfy sofas and chill atmosphere will probably entice you to lounge for a while. President Obama popped in here when he was on the campaign trail and there are lots of photos and other Obama-inspired art on the walls.

BROAD STREET CAFÉ
Durham

1116 Broad St.
Durham, NC 27705
(919) 416-9707 | www.broadstreetcafe.com
Popular restaurant and local music venue, features acts for kids on Sunday afternoons from October to March, sing-alongs, puppet shows, story time... Good kid's menu.

BRUEGGER'S BAGELS
Durham

626 9th St.
Durham, NC 27705
(919) 286-7897 | www.brueggers.com
Freshly baked bagels plus soup, fruit, brownies and cookies.

BULLOCK'S BAR-B-QUE
Durham

3330 Quebec Dr.
Durham, NC 27705
(919) 383-6202 | www.bullocksbbq.com
Southern Living raves about Bullock's. Owner Tommy Bullock displays a "Wall of Fame" with photos of all the celebs who have dined here. This is perhaps Durham's best known restaurant. Bullock's has been in operation since 1952, which also makes it Durham's longest continuously running restaurant.

CHAMAS CHURRASCARIA
Durham

Brightleaf Square/ 905 W. Main St.
Durham, NC 27701
(919) 682-1309 | www.chamas.us
Kids are intrigued by the fire torches on the outside wall... dads are intrigued by the delicious Brazilian grub.

CHUBBY'S TACOS
Durham

748 9th St.
Durham, NC 27705
(919) 286-4499 | www.chubbystacos.com
A kid favorite for cheap and easy eats, e.g. a rice and bean taco for a buck-and-a-half. Three locations in Durham, two in Raleigh. This is an easy place to become "regulars."

19

CINELLI'S
Durham

604 W. Morgan St.
Durham, NC 27701
(919) 416-4554 | www.cinellis-nc.com
Great place to grab a pizza pie and sit outside on nice days. Kids can play around in the courtyard at West Village until the food comes.

COSMIC CANTINA
Durham

1920 Perry St.
Durham, NC 27705
(919) 286-1875
Mexican cuisine. All the basics are covered: burritos, tacos, quesadillas, plus a nice selection of vegetarian options. Just around the corner from 9th Street, head upstairs toward the noise. On warm days, take advantage of the off-street back patio.

DOG HOUSE
Durham

200 Guess Rd.
Durham, NC 27705
(919) 286-9200
Eight locations in the area. Dog House has been around for 40 years. If you're here to satisfy your cravings for a classic southern chili dog, then you're barking up the right tree.

DOS PERROS
Durham

200 N. Mangum St.
Durham, NC 27701
(919) 956-2750 | www.dosperrosrestaurant.com
Voted Durham's best new restaurant and best Mexican and Latin American restaurant. All items are margarine and shortening-free.

ELMO'S DINER
Durham

776 9th St.
Durham, NC 277
(919) 416-3823 | www.elmosdiner.com
A Durham tradition. Kids color a picture of Elmo's duck mascot and mount it on the wall near the entrance. Walk in and see literally hundreds of these pictures from the hordes of young customers, and there's little doubt that you're in a family-friendly place. The best breakfast in Durham, served all day. I've never met a kid who didn't love Elmo's pancakes drenched in maple syrup.

EL RODEO
Durham

Brightleaf Square/ 905 W. Main St.
Durham, NC 27701
(919) 683-2417 | www.elrodeoofdurham.com
Quick, inexpensive Mexican grub. Sit outside in the courtyard at Bright-leaf Square and people watch while you chow down. Note: they go all out when you tell them it's your kid's birthday. Mariachi trio, etc. My youngest even got a complimentary sombrero on her birthday, which I'm thinking is just because she's so darn cute.

GREEN ROOM
Durham

1108 Broad St.
Durham, NC 27705
(919) 286-2359
Teach your kids how to drink (root) beer belly up and play classic pinball and shuffleboard. Best to get there early (around 5 pm). Great tunes on the jukebox.

FOSTER'S MARKET
Durham

2694 Durham-Chapel Hill Blvd.
Durham, NC 27707
(919) 489-3944 | www.fostersmarket.com
Gourmet grocery as well as one of the best eateries in the area, operated by foodie legend Sarah Foster (former personal chef for Martha Stewart). Great place to lounge away a Sunday. Come for brunch, stay all after-noon. Place is always hopping with Dukies and other locals. Good selection of candy, pastries and other treats as well.

FRANCESCA'S DESSERT CAFÉ
Durham

706 9th St.
Durham, NC 27705
(919) 286-4188 | www.francescasdessertcaffe.com
Chocolate-laden éclairs, fudge brownies, homemade gelato and sor-bets... located in the heart of pedestrian-friendly 9th St. Great place for dads to pop in on a cold winter day and warm up with a shot of espresso while the kids get a sugar fix.

GUGLHUPF
Durham

2706 Durham-Chapel Hill Blvd.
Durham, NC 27707
(919) 401-2600 | www.guglhupf.com
A favorite for brunch. Great fun food. A taste of Europe in our backyard. Very special around Christmas time.

LOCAL YOGURT
Durham

2501 University Dr.
Durham, NC 27707
(919) 489-5900 | www.localyogurt.com
Tasty preservative-free yogurt and bright, friendly Rockwood neighborhood hangout.

MADHATTER'S
Durham

1802 W. Main St.
Durham, NC 27701
(919) 286-1987 | www.madhattersbakeshop.com
Great place for breakfast or lunch. Excellent omelets. Best known for their baked goods; pastries, muffins, cakes, and cookies. Reliable choice for Valentine's Day goodies.

MAGGIANO'S
Durham

Streets of Southpoint/ 8030 Renaissance Pky.
Durham, NC 27713
(919) 572-0070 | www.maggianos.com
Excellent Italian entrees that come in enormous portions. I've fed my family for days on what I brought home in doggie bags.

MELLOW MUSHROOM
Durham

American Tobacco Historic District
410 Blackwell St.
Durham, NC 27701
(919) 680-8500 | www.mellowmushroom.com
Great pizza and calzones, fun atmosphere. Good choice for before or after a Bull's game.

NOODLES & CO.
Durham

2608 Erwin Dr.
Durham, NC 27705
(919) 383-5600 | www.noodles.com
Absolutely the least expensive meals I ever provide my children. They love to split a small order of plain rice noodles (which is plenty), smother it in soy sauce and call it a meal. Total damage: about $2.

POP'S AT WEST VILLAGE
Durham

605 W. Main St.
Durham, NC 27701
(919) 956-7677| www.pops-durham.com
Pops won me over when the head chef spent a good 5 minutes at our table interviewing my girls in an attempt to come up with a perfect risotto dish for them. This was on a very busy Saturday night with a line out the door, by the way. Not only was it a nice gesture, but he nailed it, resulting in two very happy little girls with full tummies and one appreciative father.

Q-SHACK
Durham

2510 University Dr.
Durham, NC 27707
(919) 402-4227
Great bbq for sure, but it's the sides that make this one of our favorites; mac and cheese, collard greens, and hush puppies. There are rolls of paper towels at every table for obvious reasons.

RANDY'S PIZZA
Durham

1813 MLK, Jr. Blvd.
Durham, NC 27707
(919) 490-6850 | www.randys-pizza.com
Delicious NY-style pizza and fast, friendly service.

SATISFACTION
Durham

Brightleaf Square
905 W. Main St.
Durham, NC 27701
(919) 682-7397 | www.satisfactionrestaurant.com
Great place to catch the big game on one of the dozens of TVs inside or dine al fresco in the courtyard. Excellent veggie burger, for the inevitable, obligatory point when your child decides to become a vegetarian (until she realizes that rules out bacon).

TOMATO JAKES
Durham

8202 Renaissance Pkwy. Ste. 101
Durham, NC 27713
(919) 572-7222 | www.tomatojakes.com
Good pizza and good fun. Kids' Night with Ted's Twisted Balloons delights the bambinos with free balloon sculptures. 5:30-7:30pm on certain nights. Call ahead to confirm.

TORERO'S MEXICAN RESTAURANT
Durham

800 W. Main St.
Durham, NC 27701
(919) 682-4197 | www.torerosmexicanrestaurants.com
A couple locations in Durham and several throughout the state, the one downtown on the corner of Main and Duke is always hopping. Great food, casual and kid-friendly. How kid-friendly? Kids eat free from the children's menu every night with the exception of Friday and Saturday. Open for lunch and dinner.

23

TWISTED NOODLES   Durham
4201-112 University Dr.
Durham, NC 27707
(919) 489-9888 | www.twistednoodles.com
The Triangle's largest offering of authentic Thai food, with locations in Durham and Chapel hill.

TYLER'S   Durham
American Tobacco Historic District
324 Blackwell St.
Durham, NC 27701
(919) 433-0345 | www.tylerstaproom.com
A good children's menu. Great homemade potato chips. My kid's favorite part: bendaroos instead of crayons to occupy their time before the food comes.

WHOLE FOODS   Durham
621 Broad St.
Durham, NC 27705
(919) 286-2290 | www.wholefoodsmarket.com/stores/durham
Excellent salad bar, pizza by the slice and a number of healthy options at the bustling downtown grocer.

WIMPY'S BURGERS AND BISCUITS   Durham
617 Hicks St.
Durham, NC 27705
(919) 286-4380
A no frills, no place to sit but tasty and inexpensive burger and onion ring joint.

CHICK-FIL-A   Garner
2720 Timber Dr.
Garner, NC 27529
(919) 661-2448 | www.chickenspace.com
On Tuesdays from 5-7:30 pm, kids make a craft and meet Mr. Cow. Plus a free kid's meal with the purchase of adult meal.

CRACKER BARREL   Garner
5199 NC 42
Garner, NC 27529
(919) 661-4044 | www.crackerbarrel.com
Old-fashioned fun and grub; play checkers, sit a spell in a rocker; buy you some peach preserves and then settle in for a mess of maple-syrup drenched pancakes and grits.

GOODBERRY'S
Garner

1407 Garner Station Blvd.
Garner, NC 27603
(919) 722-0205 | www.goodberrys.com
Goodberry's always draws a crowd with its frozen custard. The Carolina Concrete is a favorite made by mixing a custard flavor with a variety of toppings. Locations in Raleigh as well as Cary, Durham, Garner and Wake Forest.

HOMEGROWN PIZZA
Holly Springs

4928 Linksland Dr., #101
Holly Springs, NC 27540
(919) 577-5575 | homegrownpizza.com
$3.95 children's menu includes a variety of pasta, pizza and burger options.

SWEET CHEEKS
Holly Springs

313 Amacord Way
Holly Springs, NC 27540
(919) 815-3651 | www.scbakery.com
Cakes. Just like Grandma used to bake. Birthday cakes, cupcakes, sheet cakes... pies and pastries, as well. For any occasion or to simply satisfy the occasional sweet tooth cravings of you and your sweeties.

ANDY'S BURGERS, SHAKES & FRIES
Knightdale

1011 Smithfield Rd.
Knightdale, NC 27545
(919) 261-9841 | www.andysburgers.net
Kid's menu items include hamburger or cheeseburger, grilled cheese, hot dog or a four-piece chicken nugget meal (includes kid-sized fries and a soft drink). Plus, all Andy's kids' meals come served in their own special "hot rod" and include a fun toy!

MOE'S SOUTHWEST GRILL
Knightdale

1016 Shoppes of Midway Dr. Ste. A
Knightdale, NC 27545
(919) 266-1018 | www.moes.com
Fresh-Mex, Southwestern fare... inexpensive and tasty.

RUDINO'S
Knightdale

4022 Village Park Dr.
Knightdale, NC 27545
(919) 359-2871 | www.rudinos.com
Kid's menu is for 12 and under and includes drink... prices range from $2.50 to $3.95... cheese pizza, grilled cheese and chips, mac 'n cheese, chicken fingers and fries... one of a dozen or so in the Triangle.

25

ALLEN AND SON BAR-B-QUE
Pittsboro

6550 US 15-501
Pittsboro, NC 27312
(919) 542-2294

Good eastern NC style barbeque and reasonably-priced kid's menu; cash only, closed Sunday and Monday.

AL'S DINER
Pittsboro

535 West St.
Pittsboro, NC 27312
(919) 542-5808

Lots of yummy food to choose from on the menu, including tasty milkshakes and ice cream.

ANGELINA'S KITCHEN
Pittsboro

23 Rectory St.
Pittsboro, NC 27312
(919) 545-5505 | www.angelinaskitchenonline.com

Local food with a Greek twist when you have a hankering for a gyro or falafel sandwich.

CHATHAM MARKETPLACE
Pittsboro

480 Hillsboro St., Ste. 320
Pittsboro, NC 27312
(919) 542-2643 | www.chathammarketplace.coop/cafe

Local co-op grocery and café. Enjoy homemade croissants, muffins and scones.

DIANA'S TEX MEX
Pittsboro

122 Sanford Rd.
Pittsboro, NC 27312
(919) 542-5338 | www.dianastexmex.com

A dozen items on the kid's menu, each for just $3.95.

PITTSBORO GENERAL STORE CAFE
Pittsboro

39 West St.
Pittsboro, NC 27312
(919) 542-2432 | www.thegeneralstorecafe.com

Live Irish music first Saturday of each month. Burrito Bash, a fundraiser for local nonprofits, is held each Monday.

S&T'S SODA SHOPPE

Pittsboro

85 Hillsboro St.
Pittsboro, NC 27312
(919) 545-0007
Beautifully restored old-fashioned ice cream parlor located in the heart of Pittsboro. Menu includes lots of great lunch and dinner selections for grown-ups and kids. Fizzies, floats, malts, cheese dogs.... a veritable children's paradise.

VIRLIE'S GRILL

Pittsboro

58 Hillsboro St.
Pittsboro, NC 27312
(919) 542-0376
Mickey Mouse pancakes for $1.95 will make any hungry kid happy in the AM, or later.

ARMADILLO GRILL

Raleigh

439 Glenwood Ave.
Raleigh, NC 27603
(919) 546-0555 | www.armadillogrill.com
Great tacos, and no armadillos on the menu (as far as I know).

A&W RESTAURANT

Raleigh

651 E. Six Forks Rd.
Raleigh, NC 27609
(919) 836-1381 | www.awrestaurants.com
Wash down a fully-loaded cheeseburger with a frosty, frothy mug of A&W root beer.

BEAN SPROUT

Raleigh

3721 Hillsborough Rd.
Raleigh, NC 27607
(919) 755-0554
A good Chinese restaurant with fast service, generous portions and inexpensive entrées.

CAPTAIN STANLEY'S

Raleigh

3333 S. Wilmington St.
Raleigh, NC 27603
(919) 779-7878
Great hushpuppies, cole slaw and fried shrimp kind of place. Cash only. Nothing fancy, just clean and cordial and tasty food.

CARVEL
Raleigh

RDU Airport
1000 Trade DR. A-25
Raleigh, NC 27623
www.carvel.com

Famous for its selection of ice cream cakes, Carvel claims to have found 53,000 ways to "freeze your brain." Cups and cones, sundaes, smoothies, shakes, Fizzlers and various novelties. A good excuse to go to the airport even if you don't have a flight to catch.

CHAR-GRILL
Raleigh

618 Hillsborough St.
Raleigh, NC 27603
(919) 821-7636 | www.chargrillusa.com

A Raleigh icon. Locals consistently claim that Char-Grill's serves THE best hamburgers and hot dogs in town. Take out only.

CHEESECAKE FACTORY
Raleigh

4325 Glenwood Ave.
Raleigh, NC
(919) 781-0050 | www.thecheesecakefactory.com

Tiramisu, red velvet cake, carrot cake are among the 50+ tempting desert items on the menu.

DOMINIC'S NY PIZZERIA
Raleigh

5911 Poyner Village Pkwy. Ste. 105
Raleigh, NC 27616
(919) 878-7782 | www.dominicspizza.com

Owned by a dad who knows a thing or two about New York pizza. Trained as a pizza chef in his native Italy, he moved to Brooklyn where he opened a popular New York pizzeria and thankfully, for all of us here in the Triangle, decided to come south.

DOS TOQUITOS
Raleigh

106 Wilmington St.
Raleigh, NC 27601
(919) 835-3593 | www.dostoquitoscentro.com

Always a top choice for lunch whenever we're in downtown Raleigh. A Mexican restaurant that goes WAY beyond tacos and burritos.

FLYING BISCUIT
Raleigh

2016 Clark Ave.
Raleigh, NC 27605
(919) 833-6924 | www.flyingbiscuit.com

Popular breakfast, brunch and lunch spot in Cameron Village.

FAT DADDY'S

Raleigh

6201 Glenwood Ave.
Raleigh, NC 27612
(919) 787-3773
In addition to yummy food, there's free face painting and balloon art three Mondays a month from 6-8 pm. Call ahead to confirm dates.

FRANK'S PIZZA

Raleigh

2030 New Bern Ave.
Raleigh, NC 27610
(919) 231-8990
Great pizza, friendly staff. Plus, the Philly Cheese Steak is all the rage.

THE MELTING POT

Raleigh

3100 Wake Forest Rd.
Raleigh, NC 27609
(919) 878-0477 | www.meltingpot.com
What kid doesn't love to fondue? Anytime a meal is do it yourself but doesn't seem like work, kids are all over it.

MOONLIGHT PIZZA COMPANY

Raleigh

615 Morgan St.
Raleigh, NC 27603
(919) 755-9133 | www.moonlightpizza.com
Funky, urban décor. Hip pizza joint, usually an eclectic mix of fellow diners... students, young professionals and parents with their young hungry kids. Pizza plus salads, calzones, stromboli.

NEOMONDE

Raleigh

3817 Berry Rd.
Raleigh, NC 27607
(919) 828-1628 | www.neomonde.com
Kid friendly and super yummy authentic Middle Eastern food. Suggestion: take the kids to Neomonde after a visit to the NC Art Museum. Neomonde was founded 30 years ago by Lebanese brothers who came to America. Repeat customers are affectionately known as "Neomonde Nuts."

ORIENTSPIRATION

Raleigh

Falls River Town Center
10940 Raven Ridge Rd. Ste.122
Raleigh, NC 27616
(919) 846-0910 | www.orientspiration.com
Authentic Asian teas are their specialty; store also carries teapots, home decor, and other items from the Orient. A learning experience for the children where they can sample a variety of teas and snacks.

29

RALEIGHWOOD CINEMA GRILL

Raleigh

6609 Falls of Neuse Rd.
Raleigh, NC 27615
(919) 847-0326 | www.raleighwoodmovies.com
Family-owned and operated movie theater with a twist: dinner is served with the movie. Have popcorn shrimp and popcorn!

THE ROAST GRILL

Raleigh

7 S. West St.
Raleigh, NC 27603
(919) 832-8292 | www.roastgrill.com
Been around since 1940. Specializing in hot dogs, pound cake and baklava.

SNOOPY'S

Raleigh

600 Hillsborough St
Raleigh, NC 27604
919-839-2176 | www.snoopys.com
Raleigh landmark, the "original" Snoopy's opened in 1978 and they've been serving hot dogs, cheeseburgers, and foot long hot dogs with mustard, onion, and chili on a steamed bun ever since.

TOBACCO ROAD SPORTS CAFE

Raleigh

222 Glenwood Ave.
Raleigh, NC 27603
(919) 832-3688 | www.tobaccoroadsportscafe.com
A family-friendly sports restaurant, where you and the kiddos can catch the big ACC matchup from recliners or at a table. Kids eat free on Tuesdays. Another location recently opened adjacent to Bulls Stadium in Durham.

UNCLE FATTY'S DRIVE IN

Raleigh

427 Woodburn Rd.
Raleigh, NC 27605
(919) 835-0404 | www.unclefattys.net
Drive-in burger joint in west Raleigh with a kid's menu that includes burgers, dogs, milkshakes and grilled cheese, each under four bucks.

CUPS 'N CONES
ICE CREAM/COFFEE SHOPPE
Wake Forest

1839 Main St. Ste. 100
Wake Forest, NC 27587
(919) 435-0285

Ice cream cakes, fruit smoothies, cookies and muffins. Plus, fresh brewed espresso drinks for dad, a perfect nightcap to a busy day at the Factory.

SWEET LORALEE PASTRIES
Wake Forest

1839 Main St. Ste. 112
Wake Forest, NC 27587
(919) 453-1024 | www.sweetloralee.com

From patty cakes to dirt cakes with gummy worms, Sweet Loralee's is the place for all your fun, tasty pastry needs in Wake Forest.

THE BEST DAD/CHILD
ACTIVITIES

ACTIVITIES

DREAMSPORTS CENTER   Apex

1016 Investment Blvd.
Apex, NC 27502
(919) 387-2955 | www.dreamsportscenter.com
Ice hockey, soccer, leagues, classes: "a place where everyone gets to play..." For both kids and grownups (because dads want to play too).

HOPPER'S HOUSE   Apex

1500 Town Side Dr., Ste. 100
Apex, NC 27502
(919) 363-3109 | www.thehoppershouse.com
Bounce house, rock wall, basketball. For kids 10 and under. Expect your kiddos to sleep well after a day at Hoppers.

THE ARTS CENTER   Carrboro

300-G E. Main St.
Carrboro, NC 27510
(919) 929-2787 | www.artscenterlive.org
Wonderful ambiance and great music and theater for a parents and kids. Check website for performances and info on children's theater and music, art and other classes for kids.

CARR MILL MALL   Carrboro

200 N. Greensboro Street
Carrboro, NC 27510
(919) 942-8669 | www.carrmillmall.com
Carr Mill Mall is a beautifully restored former textile mill (built in 1899 as Alberta Mill and listed on the National Register of Historic Places), which houses many specialty stores, restaurants, a chocolate shop, boutiques and galleries. Did I mention the chocolate shop?

BUFFALOE LANES   Cary

151 High House Rd.
Cary, NC 27511
(919) 468-8684 | www.buffaloelanes.com
Bowling anyone? Smoke and alcohol-free bowling for the whole family. Also a couple Buffaloe alleys in Raleigh.

BULLWINKLE'S FAMILY FOOD 'N FUN   Cary

1040 Buck Jones Rd.
Cary, NC 27511
(919) 319-7575 www.bullwinkles.com
Offers a climbing wall, arcade games, and an indoor playground with three slides. Birthday parties can be arranged any day of the week. But do you think any kid knows who Bullwinkle is?

CARY PUBLIC LIBRARY
Cary

310 South Academy St.
Cary, NC 27511
(919) 460-3350
Houses more than 115,000 volumes and features an array of monthly children's programs.

GYMBOREE PLAY AND MUSIC CENTER
Cary

210 Colonades Way #D
Cary, NC 27511
(919) 267-4762 | www.gymboree.com
Toddler music, physical play and safe exercise programs for little ones.

PARTY MACHINE
Cary

1313 Buck Jones Rd.
Cary, NC 27606
(919) 468-1080
The play area for children 7 years and under has a pretend office, log cabin, kitchen, puppets and a stage, arts and crafts activities and a game room. Plus, they've got a café area for dad.

THE LITTLE GYM
Cary

1241 NW Maynard Rd.
Cary, NC 27513
(919) 300-7345 | www.thelittlegymraleigh-carync.com
Professionally-developed, non-competitive program designed to build motor skills in a fun, nurturing environment.

TRIANGLE AQUATIC CENTER
Cary

275 Convention Dr.
Cary, NC 27511
(919) 459-4045 | www.triangleaquatics.org
The largest public aquatic facility in North Carolina features a 50-meter competition pool, a 25-yard training pool, and a warm-water instructional pool. 72,000 square foot facility. Take swim lessons at the Center through the Triangle Swim Club.

TRIANGLE SWIM SCHOOL
Cary

275 Convention Dr.
Cary, NC 27511
(919) 267-4762 | www.triangleswimschool.com
Learn to swim at the school affiliated with the Triangle Aquatic Center. Featuring low student ratios, knowledgeable instructors and personal attention. Because dads should leave the task of teaching their kid how to swim to the pros.

35

ACKLAND ART MUSEUM
Chapel Hill

1015 Columbia St.
Chapel Hill, NC
(919) 966-5736 | www.ackland.org
The museum's collection consists of more than 16,000 works, featuring NC's premier collection of Asian art. Free admission. Closed Mondays and Tuesdays.

ART WITH EVAN
Chapel Hill

120 Old Durham Rd.
Chapel Hill, NC 27517
(919) 968-0642 | www.artwithevan.com
Summer camps, half-day painting workshops, Friday night painting workshops and art parties... this atmosphere is creative, positive and nurturing. At Art with Evan, colorful impressionist artwork surrounds students in a calm, sunlit studio. Mozart, Bach, or Vivaldi plays as your little Picasso is inspired to paint and draw from still-life, animals, the figure, landscape, or their imaginations. Drop-ins welcome. Call for times.

CELY'S HOUSE
Chapel Hill

Chapel Hill, NC 27514
(919) 929-3591 | www.celyshouse.com
Cely's House offers creative arts after school programs, pottery handbuilding and wheel classes for small groups, birthday parties and summer camp classes, too.

C'EST SI BON COOKING SCHOOL
Chapel Hill

U1002 Brace Ln.
Chapel Hill, NC 27516
(919) 942-6550 www.cestsibon.net
Cooking school where kids can learn to cook for their hungry dads.

COMMUNITY CLAY STUDIO
Chapel Hill

200 Plan Rd.
Chapel Hill, NC 27514
(919) 968-2793
Try your hand at pottery at this well-equipped studio with eight pottery wheels and three kilns. Don't just buy Grandma a gift, make her something!

KUDZU CHILDREN'S MUSEUM
Chapel Hill

105 E. Franklin St.
Chapel Hill, NC 27514
(919) 933-1455 | www.kidzuchildrensmuseum.org
Engaging, hands-on exhibits and programs to inspire young children (up to age 8) to learn through play. Check out their Laughing Turtle Gift Shop.

36

LOWE'S HARDWARE
LITTLE BUILDER'S CLINIC Chapel Hill

1801 Chapel Hill Blvd
Chapel Hill, NC 27514
(919) 967-3289

One Saturday each month a Lowe's expert teaches a few simple skills and kids complete a seasonal craft.

AMERICAN TOBACCO
HISTORIC DISTRICT Durham

318 Blackwell St.
Durham, NC 277
(919) 433-1566 | www.americantobaccohistoricdistrict.com

Lots of restaurants, including Mellow Mushroom and Tyler's Tap Room, both of which have fantastic kid's menus (and cool plastic cups to take home to add to your collection). American Tobacco is known for the river than runs through it and the huge lawn which makes it not only a dinner destination but a place to spend an evening with the kids, especially during summer when the popular Concert on the Lawn series kicks in. Across the street from Bull's baseball stadium.

AMERICAN TOBACCO TRAIL Durham

Durham, NC
www.triangletransit.org/ATT

A safe, easy fun place for kids to learn and enjoy bike riding. The 22 mile trail snakes through parts of Durham, Chatham and Wake Counties. Check out the website to learn easy points of entrée.

AMF DURHAM LANES Durham

4508 Durham-Chapel Hill Blvd.
Durham, NC 27707
(919) 489-9154 | www.amf.com
32 Lanes of family fun, plus a snack bar and arcade.

BRIGHTLEAF SQUARE Durham

Corner of W. Main St. and S. Gregson St.
Durham, NC 27701
(919) 682-9229 | www.historicbrightleaf.com

Another one of those massive renovated tobacco warehouses Durham is famous for. Includes a used bookstore, music store, upscale and funky clothing stores and some of the more popular restaurants in town. The open court yard is great for rollerblading or dancing with your buddies whenever the Friday night concerts are in season (all Summer). The gelato at Amelia's is scrumptious.

BULL CITY CARRIAGE CO.   Durham
Corner of Main St. and Gregson St.
Durham, NC 27701
(919) 730-7586
Horse-drawn carriage offers 20-30 minute tours around Durham's downtown Brightleaf Square district and Duke's East Campus. Cost is $9 per person (or $15 per couple). Kids ride free.

BULL CITY CONNECTOR   Durham
(919) 485-RIDE | www.bullcityconnector.org
Free shuttle which serves downtown. Picks up every fifteen minutes at stops every few blocks from Golden Belt to Duke University, mostly along Main Street. Sometimes, my girls and I hop on just for the ride. Or we hop off near the downtown Public Library for a while and then head out to Duke Gardens for an afternoon picnic... without getting in the car. A great way to see the city in a clean, brand spanking new hybrid bus.

THE BULL STATUE AT CCB PLAZA   Durham
201 N. Corcoran St.
Durham, NC 27701
(919) 560-4355
CCB Plaza is an open-air gathering place smack in the center of downtown, home to the bronze bull statue named Major. Brochures claim the statue is "life-sized." If that's true, that is one big bull. Great photo opp. Fun to climb on and dangle from his horns. Keep in mind that this bull is very realistic and well-endowed. Be prepared to explain bull anatomy. Venue hosts evening concert series and other special events throughout the year.

CHUCK E CHEESE   Durham
3724 Mayfair St.
Durham, NC27707
(919) 493-6084 | www.chuckecheese.com
Where a kid can be a kid (and a dad can keep track of tokens and tickets and prizes).

DANCE THEATRE SOUTH   Durham
Sutton Station
5832 Fayetteville Rd. Ste. 110
Durham, NC 27713
(919) 361-7006 | www.dancetheatresouth.com
A family dance studio serving the Raleigh/Durham area which offers top-notch programs that build confidence and promote fun.

DOLLAR GENERAL
Durham

800 Broad St.
Durham, NC 27705
(919) 416-1303

I like to give my girls $3 each and let them get anything they want. What's amazing is the cool swag six bucks can buy and how much fun they have in the process.

DOWNTOWN FARMER'S MARKET
Durham

501 Foster St. (the Pavilion at Central Park)
Durham, NC 27701
(919) 667-3099 | www.durhamfarmersmarket.com

A great place to grab delectable home grown veggies and sample local jams and honey. Local artisans usually have booths selling their wares as well. Chances are your kid will see somebody they know and take off to play in the park across the street when they get bored with the fruits and veggies. Hours vary by season, so check the website.

DUKE HOMESTEAD
Durham

2828 Duke Homestead Rd.
Durham, NC 27705
(919) 477-5498 | www.nchistoricsites.org/duke

Early home, farm and factories of Washington Duke, tobacco pioneer, philanthropist and Durham legend. Check out the cigarette museum (or not, depending on how you want to tread those waters). Interesting education in the role of tobacco in shaping this part of the world.

DUKE LEMUR CENTER
Durham

3705 Erwin Rd.
Durham, NC 27705
(919) 489-3364 | www.lemur.duke.edu

Can't make it to Madagascar? Well, there's a little bit of Madagascar nestled on 85 acres adjacent to Duke's campus. Home to about 250 animals, including 233 lemurs as well as lorises from India and bush babies from Africa. Call in advance to arrange a tour.

DURHAM ARTS COUNCIL
Durham

120 Morris St.
Durham, NC 27701
(919) 560-2787 | www.durhamarts.org

Summer art camps for ages 5-12. Over 700 courses are taught each year in drawing, painting, writing, dance, clay, sculpture. Also home to the Durham Art Walk (www.durhamartwalk.com) held twice a year, usually in March and November, which features the goods of over 200 artists, starts at DAC and sprawls through downtown and Golden Belt.

39

ACTIVITIES

DURHAM COUNTY MAIN LIBRARY
Durham

300 North Roxboro St.
Durham, NC 27701
(919) 560-0100 | www.durhamcountylibrary.org

Durham's largest library houses more than 466,000 books including more than 100,000 children's books. They have regular story time and art and craft activities as well. Visit the website for details.

FUN ZONE
Durham

101 Orange St.
Durham, NC 27701
(919) 683-1582 | www.thefunzoneforkids.com

This is a place downtown where you can drop off your kids for a couple hours and they can have fun and be supervised by a responsible adult while you catch a show at DPAC or enjoy a special grown up dinner. The space is also available for rent for birthday parties. Think games, toys, crafts and a bouncy house.

GIRLS ROCK
Durham

Durham, NC
www.girlsrocknc.org

For girls ages 7-17. Nonprofit organization that encourages girls to be confident, creative members of their communities. Girls form bands and participate in workshops on teamwork, body confidence, zine-making, DIY clothing, recording, Tech Talk and more.

GOLDEN BELT
Durham

807 E. Main St.
Durham, NC 27701
(919) 967-7700 | www.goldenbeltarts.com

The renovated textile building just east of downtown is home to a number of art studios that offer classes for kids. Each third Friday of the month, the place is abuzz with art lovers. There is usually live music, food and drink and dozens of studios open to the public with artists eager to answer questions from inquiring youngsters.

HAYTI HERITAGE CENTER
Durham

804 Old Fayetteville St.
Durham, NC 27701
(919) 683-1709 | www.hayti.org

Located in the former St. Joseph's AME Church, a National Historic Landmark, the Hayti Heritage Center is operated by the St. Joseph's Historic Foundation. Features art gallery exhibits, summer camps, Kwanzaa celebration, jazz, R&B, gospel music... provides a great mix of quality cultural arts programs for kids and grownups alike.

HISTORIC STAGVILLE

Durham

5826 Old Oxford Hwy.
Durham, NC 27712
(919) 620-0120 | www.historicstagvillefoundation.org
Tour the largest antebellum plantation in the state.

HOOPS CITY U

Durham

4300 Emperor Blvd., Suite 250
Durham, NC 27703
(919) 474-2400 | www.hoopscityu.com
A state of the art 25,000 square foot basketball training facility offering leagues, teams, and individual instruction for ages four and up. It is never too early to perfect the turn-around jump shot and crossover dribble.

KARATE INTERNATIONAL OF DURHAM

Durham

5324 New Hope Commons Blvd.
Durham, NC 27707
(919) 489-6100 | www.kidurham.com
Karate, judo, jujitsu, kendo and self-defense classes for kids and adults. Summer camp is also available.

LOCO POPS

Durham

2600 Hillsborough Rd.
Durham, NC 277
(919) 286-3500 | www.ilovelocopops.com
Not so much a hidden jewel since it was featured on NPR, but nothing says Durham like Loco Pops. These Mexican-style popsicles swept the city a few years ago and should still be considered one of the best things about Durham. Don't be afraid to try some of the funky (even downright bizarre) experimental flavors.

MICHAEL'S

Durham

5422 New Hope Commons Dr.
Durham. NC 27701
(919) 490-4945 | www.Michaels.com
National chain offers craft supplies, classes, craft parties, and a weekly crafting club for kids on Saturday mornings.

MUSIC EXPLORIUM

Durham

5314 Hwy 55, Ste. 107
Durham, NC 27713
(919) 484-9090 | www.musicexplorium.com
Drum clubs, rhythm circles and hands-on music events. This is a unique birthday party venue. Guaranteed to get your child's head bopping and feet tapping.

ACTIVITIES

41

MUSIC ON THE LAWN AT AMERICAN TOBACCO

Durham

318 Blackwell St.
Durham, NC 277
(919) 433-1566
www.americantobaccohistoricdistrict.com/events-and-exhibits.html

On a dozen or so Friday nights from April to October each year, American Tobacco teams with WUNC-FM and its popular Back Porch Music series and puts on what has quickly become one of the most popular outings in the Triangle. The lawn is always packed with adults sipping wine and sprawled on blankets while kids find old friends or make new ones and dance and run and play ball and then cool off by sticking their toes – and hopefully that's all – in the river that runs through the campus. High quality regional and national acts. Plenty of food and drink options on-site.

NASHER MUSEUM OF ART

Durham

2001 Campus Dr.
Durham, NC 27705
(919) 684-5135 | www.nasher.duke.edu

Beautiful on-campus museum with leading-edge exhibitions, dynamic programs, Family Days, 65,000 square feet of exhibits and a swanky café. Free admission on Thursdays from 5-9 pm.

NC MUSEUM OF LIFE AND SCIENCE

Durham

433 W. Murray Ave.
Durham, NC 27704
(919) 220-5429 | www.ncmls.org

Dig for dinosaur bones, ride the train and visit the farm animals. Our favorite is the butterfly house where, if you are patient enough, one of the hundreds of exotic butterflies might land on your shoulder or cheek. A great place to warm up on cold days. We like to pretend we're in a tropical rain forest. Free on Wednesdays. But, if you're a local you'll want to buy a membership. My girls would go here every day if we could.

NORTHGATE MALL

Durham

1058 W. Club Blvd.
Durham, NC 27701
(919) 286-4400 | www.northgatemall.com

Fun place to hang out with the kids, especially on cold or rainy days when you can't be outside. Take in a movie or ride the carousel, bungee jump or visit Santa and ride his train during Christmas time.

REI

Durham

6911 Fayetteville Rd (Southpoint Mall)
Durham, NC 27713
(919) 806-3442 | www.rei.com/stores/85
Outdoor gear store opens their climbing wall to kids (and parents) on Thursdays and Saturdays.

SCRAP EXCHANGE

Durham

548 Foster St.
Durham, NC
(919) 688-6960 | www.scrapexchange.org
Want a unique, handmade gift for mom on Mother's Day? Spend a couple bucks and a few hours at the Scrap Exchange. Pick from barrels and barrels of "one man's junk" then head to the art room where you'll find scissors and glue and tape and whatever your little one needs to assemble a masterpiece. Hours are 11 AM to 5 PM from Wednesday to Friday, 11 AM to 6 PM on Thursday and 10 AM to 5 PM on Saturday.

SEA OF LEARNING AT NORTHGATE MALL

Durham

1058 W. Club Blvd.
Durham, NC 27701
(919) 286-2522
A Sea of Learning hosts "FISH-TALES" (story-time) every Thursday morning at 10:30 AM. Fish-Tales is designed for ages 2-5, although younger and older siblings are welcome! Sing, read, do "finger-plays" and always have a craft to make. Free.

SEW CRAFTY

Durham

104 Parrish St.
Durham, NC 27701
(919) 683-1582
Learn to sew, paint a flower pot, make polymer clay beads and barrettes or have a crafty birthday party.

SHELL'S YOGA KIDS

Durham

Durham, NC
(919) 475-6610 | www.shellsyogakids.com
Yoga classes for children ages three to 12, including classes for children with special needs. Call Michelle for private classes.

STRAWBERRY FESTIVAL
Durham

Old North Durham Park
724 Foster St.
Durham, NC 27701
www.cpsnc.org/strawberry

A berry good time; this festival has face painting, jumpee houses, live music and, of course, all things strawberry. Held every May (when the strawberries are ripe and delicious) as a fundraiser for Central Park School.

TK'S JUNGLE
Durham

4300 Emperor Blvd., Ste 250
Durham, NC 27703
(919) 474-2499 | www.tksjungle.com

A rainforest-themed indoor inflatable jump zone... jump, slide and climb on the most extensive 22-ft. inflatables in the area.

VERTICAL EDGE CLIMBING CENTER
Durham

Off US 70, 1.5 miles east of Miami Blvd.
Durham, NC
(919) 596-6910 | www.verticaledgeclimbing.com

You know they can climb on the sofa and can some times drive YOU up a wall, might as well let them try Vertical Edge. Kids receive instruction and equipment. They'll host lockins, sleepovers and birthday parties, too. Special rates for kids under 12. Call ahead for reservations for groups and info on classes.

WHEELS
Durham

715 N. Hoover Rd.
Durham, NC 277
(919) 598-1944 | www.wheelsfunparkdurham.com

A Durham landmark. It's been around forever. Features a 6,500 square foot indoor play gym with slides, ball pits, climbing structure and ropes guaranteed to wear out any child. I bring my laptop and sit at the table and get a little work done while the kiddies are in clear view. Keep in mind, this is one of those places where dozens of kids take off their shoes and climb and sweat... bring hand sanitizer. Think McDonald's Playland on steroids. Also on-site is a roller skating rink, mini golf course, batting cage, picnic areas and more. Mondays and Tuesdays are reserved for groups. Most days Wheels is open from 11 am to 10 pm and make it a point to be open when the local school system is closed for any reason. My girls would be happy to spend the entire day there.

WONDERLAND ENRICHMENT ARTS
Durham

1101 W. Main St. Suite C
Durham, NC 27701
(919) 687-0668 | www.wonderlandarts.com
Offers a variety of enrichment activities for children 6 weeks through 6 years, plus a parents' night out program on Friday evenings called Kids Cinemagic. Close to Duke's East Campus.

BURWELL SCHOOL HISTORIC SITE
Hillsborough

319 N. Churchton St.
Hillsborough, NC 27278
(919) 732-7451 | www.burwellschool.org
Docent-led tours teach kids about life at the school for young women (1837-57), and home to the Burwell family. Fun times for history and Civil War buffs.

MAPLE VIEW FARMS
Hillsborough

3109 Dairyland Rd.
Hillsborough, NC 27278
(919) 933-3600 | www.mapleviewfarm.com
400 acre dairy farm where you can sample their world famous ice cream and take a hay ride tour of the place. A very popular field trip destination for schools throughout the area. Don't forget to check out the talented ladder-climbing goats. The farm truly comes alive during Harvest. Great pumpkin patch.

OCCANEECHI INDIAN VILLAGE
Hillsborough

Foot of Cameron St. (on the Eno River)
Hillsborough, NC 27278
(919) 304-3723 | www.occaneechi-saponi.org
The Occaneechi Village sits along the banks of the Eno River near Hillsborough. It was one of the last palisaded American Indian villages visited by European explorers in the latter part of the 1600s. The current site displays an information kiosk, a portion of the log palisade wall and two historically accurate dwellings that were used by the Occaneechi ancestors.

HOLLY SPRINGS
CULTURAL CENTER
Holly Springs

300 W. Ballentine St.
Holly Springs, NC
(919) 567-4000 | www.hollyspringsnc.us/dept/park/culture
Center for arts, entertainment and special events in Holly Springs.

TRIANGLE ROCK CLUB
Morrisville

Pheasant Wood Ct.
Morrisville, NC 27560
(919) 463-7625 | www.trianglerockclub.com
The Triangle Rock Club is an indoor rock climbing center and gym. The state-of-the-art facility offers both lead and top rope climbing, bouldering, and a comprehensive fitness center.

THE SHOPS AT FEARRINGTON
Pittsboro

2000 Fearrington Village Ctr.
Pittsboro, NC 27312
(919) 542-2121 | www.theshopsatfearrington.com
A community located on an historic farm near Chapel Hill, at the heart of which is the Village Center with boutique shops, gourmet restaurants and an independent bookstore surrounded by extensive gardens and pastures; truly a place where town and country intertwine and worth a visit with the kids some Saturday afternoon.

ABRAKADOODLE
Raleigh

Raleigh, NC
(336) 270-6307 | www.abrakadoodle.com/nc03
Abrakadoodle inspires the artist in every child. The national mobile arts education program meets both the National and State Standards for visual arts education.

ADVENTURE LANDING
Raleigh

3311 Capitol Blvd.
Raleigh, NC 27604
(919) 872-1688 | www.adventurelanding.com
Over 100 interactive arcade games, a twisting quarter-mile go-kart track, nine batting cages, three 18-hole miniature golf courses and laser tag. Eery Friday night is Family Night.

ARTSPACE
Raleigh

201 E. Davie St.
Raleigh, NC 27601
(919) 821-2787 | www.artspacenc.org
A very diverse, non-profit gallery run by the artists; Artspace is a great place to visit on First Friday!

ARTSPLOSURE
Raleigh

336 Fayetteville Street Mall Ste. 405
Raleigh, NC 27601
(919) 832-8699 | www.artsplosure.org
Produces a series of festivals and events in Raleigh such as First Night Raleigh, Kidsplosure and Raleigh Arts Festival; best to check their website periodically to learn what's coming up next.

46

ARTS TOGETHER
Raleigh

114 St. Mary's St.
Raleigh, NC 27605
(919) 828-1713 | www.artstogether.org
Nonprofit multi-media school with a rich blend of classes in art, dance, drama, voice, Pilates and yoga for kids ages 3-18 and adults.

CAMERON VILLAGE
Raleigh

1900 Cameron St.
Raleigh, NC 27605
(919) 821-1350 | www.shopcameronvillage.com
You can find just about anything a dad and kid could want at Cameron Village. There is tons of great food and stores. Tree-lined walkways give it a true village feel.

CAMERON VILLAGE LIBRARY
Raleigh

1930 Clark Ave.
Raleigh, NC 27605
(919) 856-6710
www.wakegov.com/libraries/locations/cameronvillage/default.htm
Consistently recognized as one of the top libraries in the Triangle. With an excellent computer lab, children's programs, café and occasional live entertainment, it feels more like a posh bookstore than a public library.

CAPITAL CITY BICYCLE MOTOCROSS RACE TRACK
Raleigh

576 Dennis Ave.
Raleigh, NC 27603
(919) 834-4269
Open to the public, BMX track races are organized according to age groups and skills level. Hours vary, call for details. If your kid isn't quite ready to ride, it's still a fun activity to watch.

CHAVIS PARK
Raleigh

505 MLK, Jr. Blvd.
Raleigh, NC 27601
(919) 831-6968
The original 1937 carousel still runs for $1 at the historic 37-acre park.

FRANKIE'S OF RALEIGH
Raleigh

11190 Fun Park Dr.
Raleigh, NC 27617
(919) 433-7888 | www.frankiesfunpark.com/raleigh
Go-Karts, miniature golf, bumper boats, laser tag, batting cages and an awesome arcade. Pay as you play (no admission fee). Open every day and extra late.

47

ACTIVITIES

GRAND SLAM USA
Raleigh

4500 Western Blvd. #100
Raleigh, NC 27606
(919) 233-7522 grandslamusa.biz

Grand Slam USA is sure to score a hit with teens and tweens as well as younger kids. This entertainment mecca offers mini-golf, a batting cage, laser tag, bumper cars and a video arcade.

GYMCAROLINA GYMNASTICS ACADEMY
Raleigh

9321 Leesville Rd.
Raleigh, NC 27613
(919) 848-7988 | www.gymncarolina.com

Gymcarolina offers classes for all different age groups and abilities, babies to teens, beginner to advanced, and competitive team.

JAYCEE COMMUNITY CENTER
Raleigh

2405 Wade Ave.
Raleigh, NC 27607
(919) 831-6833

The Jaycee Community Center offers programs and classes for children, adults, and families. It features tennis courts, sand volleyball and ball fields.

JELLYBEANS SKATE CENTER
Raleigh

1120 Buck Jones Rd.
Raleigh, NC 27606
(919) 467-5283 | www.skatejellybeans.com

A fun family skate facility with a hardwood skate surface, snack bar and video games and as good a place as any to show off your fancy disco skating moves from back in the day.

KAZOOM CHILDREN'S THEATRE
Raleigh

431 Peace St.
Raleigh, NC
(919) 365-0555

A participatory theatre where children get to be the stars or puppeteers. Each show features a fairy tale or holiday story with lots of music, movement and interaction. For ages 2-7. Shows on Wednesdays and Thursdays at 10 am and 11 am by Carolina Puppets (see www.carolinapuppets.com). Admission is $3 for everyone over 12 months old.

MARBLES KIDS MUSEUM
Raleigh

201 East Hargett Street
Raleigh, NC 27601
919.834.4040 | www.marbleskidsmuseum.org

Marbles Kids Museum (formerly known as Exploris) inspires imagination, discovery and learning...plus it has an awesome IMAX theater. Why Marbles? A wall that wraps around the museum is filled with more than one million of them that light up at night. And Marbles is a nickname for brains. I'd say someone was using theirs when they came up with the clever name. This is another of those places your kid will want to come back to over and over and won't want to leave when they do come.

MEREDITH COLLEGE
Raleigh

3800 Hillsborough St.
Raleigh, NC 27601
(919)760-8334 | www.meredith.edu

In addition to a wide range of community events every year, the downtown Raleigh college offers a swimming program for kids ages three to 13.

MONKEY JOE'S PARTIES AND PLAY
Raleigh

6220 Glenwood Ave, Suite 104
Raleigh, NC 27612
(919) 510-6979 | www.monkeyjoes.com/Raleigh

A popular inflatable play destination and party venue, Monkey Joe's offers walk-in play time seven days a week, as well as party times. Yummy pizza too.

MORDECAI HISTORIC PARK
Raleigh

1 Mimosa St.
Raleigh, NC 27604
(919) 857-4364 | www.raleighnc.gov/mordecai

Home to Mordecai House, an antebellum plantation house, and a village street of historic structures including the birthplace of President Andrew Johnson.

THE MUSICIANS LEARNING CENTER
Raleigh

186 Wind Chime Ct. Ste. 102
Raleigh, NC
(919) 845-6770 | www.themusicianslearningcenter.com

The Musicians Learning Center offers private lessons in clarinet, flute, guitar, piano, and saxophone taught by a staff of professional musicians.

49

ACTIVITIES

NC MUSEUM OF ART AND MUSEUM PARK
Raleigh

2110 Blue Ridge Rd.
Raleigh, NC 27607
(919) 839-6262 | www.ncartmuseum.org
The popular museum has a collection that spans more than 5,000 years, from Ancient Egypt to the present.

NC MUSEUM OF HISTORY
Raleigh

5 E. Edenton St.
Raleigh, NC 27601
(919) 807-7900 | www.ncmuseumofhistory.org
Learn about the Wright Brother's flight at Kitty Hawk, the first gold mine in the US, the first African American woman to earn a college degree and all things historic about the Tar Heel State.

NC MUSEUM OF NATURAL SCIENCES
Raleigh

11 W. Jones St.
Raleigh, NC 27601
(919) 733 7450 | www.naturalsciences.org
The state's oldest museum. Four floors of hands-on, real-life exhibits, including a huge dinosaur on the 3rd floor (ok, maybe the dinosaur isn't real-life). The Discovery room has animal costumes, live bees, animal fossils, artifacts and toys. Across from the State Capitol and the History Museum. Admission is free.

NC SPORTS HALL OF FAME
Raleigh

5 E. Edenton St.
Raleigh, NC 27601
(919) 845-3455 | www.ncshof.org
Free admission. From b-ball to soccer to stock car racing, North Carolina has a rich history in sports and the museum is a great way to soak it all in with your little jocks. Located at the NC Museum of History.

NC STATE FAIR
Raleigh

1025 Blue Ridge Rd.
Raleigh, NC 27607
(919) 821-7400 | www.ncstatefair.org
Runs for a couple weeks every October... carnival rides, petting zoo, livestock competition, pig races, largest watermelon contest, fried cheese, funnel cake, cotton candy, alligator tail... Life doesn't get much better than this.

NC STATE CAPITOL
Raleigh

1 E Edenton St.
Raleigh, NC 27601
(919) 733-4994 | www.ncstatecapitol.org
Built in 1840, the state capitol building is beautiful and worthy of a brief tour... ask your guide about ghosts and legends, secret tunnels, hidden rooms and the whiskey barrel mystery.

NORTH HILLS
Raleigh

Lassiter Mill Rd. and North Hills Ave.
Raleigh, NC 27619
(919) 881-1146 | www.northhillsraleigh.com
Outdoor shopping, dining, and entertainment district.

NORTH RALEIGH ARTS & CREATIVE THEATRE
Raleigh

7713-51 Lead Mine Rd.
Raleigh, NC 27613
(919) 866-0228 | www.nract.org
A non-profit community theater that offers performing arts classes and summer camp programs for children ages five and up.

NORTH RALEIGH GYMNASTICS
Raleigh

5400 Atlantic Springs Rd.
Raleigh, NC 27616
(919) 790-9400 | www.northraleighgymnastics.com
This gym offers classes for kids beginning at the tender age of one, in addition to birthday party options (ages four and up) and camp programs. This gym has been in operation for a quarter century and prides itself on sound teaching progressions and safe, fun gymnastic opportunities for children.

OPTIMIST COMMUNITY CENTER
Raleigh

5900 Whittier Dr.
Raleigh, NC 27609
(919) 870-2880
Tennis courts, swimming pool, walking trails, and ball fields.

OPTIMIST POOL
Raleigh

5902 Whittier Dr.
Raleigh, NC 27609
(919) 870-2882
A year-round aquatic facility operated by the city of Raleigh, where you can enjoy a lap pool as well as a wading pool for the youngest swimmers.

ACTIVITIES

POLAR ICE HOUSE
Raleigh

1410 Buck Jones Rd.
Raleigh, NC 27606
(919) 460-2756 | www.cary.pucksystems.com
Great place for your future ice skater or NHL star to master skating skills.

PROGRESS ENERGY CENTER
FOR THE PERFORMING ARTS
Raleigh

2 East South St.
Raleigh, NC 27601
(919) 831-6060 | www.progressenergycenter.com
Sprinkled in the theater, opera, ballet and concerts you get kid shows like Thomas the Train on Stage! A beautiful, intimate downtown theater.

PUMP IT UP
Raleigh

10700 World Trade Blvd.
Raleigh, NC 27617
(919) 828-3344 | www.pumpitupparty.com
Massive inflatable party zone. In the immortal words of Van Halen: you might as well jump!

RALEIGH CHESS ACADEMY
Raleigh

10930 Raven Ridge Rd. Ste. 105
Raleigh, NC 27614
(919) 272-8017 | www.raleighchessacademy.com
Chess camps and chess lessons in addition to hosting monthly chess tournaments. The facility also offers free open play sessions on Friday afternoons.

RALEIGH FLUTE CHOIR
Raleigh

3809 Midlakes Dr.
Raleigh, NC 27612
(919) 787-4142 | www.raleighflutes.org
Instruments range from the piccolo to the contrabass flute (if you stretch it all the way out, you'd have around eight and a half feet of tubing!). They play a wide variety of music from classical, contemporary compositions for flute choirs and even theme songs from TV shows.

RALEIGH ICEPLEX
Raleigh

2601 N. Raleigh Blvd.
Raleigh, NC 27604
(919) 878-9002 | www.iceplex.com
The place to be for year-round ice-skating fun. Popular birthday party place. Great place to escape the sultry dog days of summer in the Triangle.

RALEIGH LITTLE THEATER

Raleigh

301 Pogue St.
Raleigh, NC 27607
(919) 821-4579 | www.raleighlittletheater.org
Musicals, comedies and dramas with local performers and guest directors. They also offer acting classes.

RALEIGH SCHOOL OF BALLET

Raleigh

3921 Beryl Rd.
Raleigh, NC 27607
(919) 834-9261 | www.raleighdance.org
The Raleigh School of Ballet offers classes for all ages and levels, from creative movement classes for the littlest dancers to professional standard ballet training for aspiring ballerinas. Affiliate school of the Raleigh Dance Theatre.

SERTOMA ARTS CENTER

Raleigh

1400 West Millbrook Rd.
Raleigh, NC 27612
(919) 420-2329
Programming includes painting, drawing, pottery, crafts, photography, dance, healing arts and more to youth, teens and adults.

STATE FARMERS MARKET

Raleigh

1201 Agriculture St.
Raleigh, NC 27603
(919) 733-7417 | www.ncfarmfresh.com
Also known as the Raleigh Farmers Market, one of five farmers markets owned by the state of North Carolina. The market encompasses 75 acres of yummy homegrown goodies.

RDU OBSERVATION DECK

RDU

RDU Airport, NC 27623
www.rdu.com/whileatairport/obpark.htm
Watch jets take off and land at the airport's observation deck, which overlooks RDU's longest runway.

CLAY FUSION

Wake Forest

1839 South Main St.
Wake Forest, NC 27587
(919) 969-0074 | www.clayfusion.com
A store where you are the artist! Enjoy time creating with your kids: painting your own pottery, working with clay, designing mosaics or beading jewelry.

53

ACTIVITIES

DELICIOUS SKATEBOARD SHOP/PARK
Wake Forest

1839 South Main St. Ste. 500
Wake Forest, NC 27587
(919) 453-1225 | www.deliciousskateboard.com
100% skater owned and operated. The shop is packed with skater goods and the Skate park is behind the main building at the Factory. 25,000 square feet of indoor and outdoor skating space, and even an upstairs area for beginners, perfect for trying out your new purchases. Beginner lessons, birthday parties and summer camps are available and all skill levels are welcome.

DESTINY DANCE INSTITUTE
Wake Forest

1839 South Main St., Ste. 374
Wake Forest, NC 27587
(919) 453-1453 | www.destinydanceinstitute.com
Ballet, point, tap, jazz, hip-hop and lyrical dance instruction for ages 4 to adult.

THE FACTORY
Wake Forest

1839 South Main St.
Wake Forest, NC 27587
(919) 453-1839 | www.eatshopplay.com
Located in historic Wake Forest, the Factory offers a dynamic mix of specialty shopping, dining, sports, entertainment and activities for the entire family.

FACTORY GO KARTS AND MINI GOLF
Wake Forest

1839 South Main St., Ste. 600
Wake Forest, NC 27587
(919) 453-2791 | www.southmainspeedway.com
If you've got a need for speed, be sure to check out this place.

JUMPIN BEANS
Wake Forest

1839 South Main St.
Wake Forest, NC 27587
(919) 521-4445 | www.jumpinbeanswakeforest.com
Jumpin Beans is an inflatable play space that offers open play, all day, every day, plus pizza, salads and snacks.

54

KLOK'S SCHOOL OF
MARTIAL ARTS

Wake Forest

1839 South Main St., Ste. 330
Wake Forest, NC 27587
(919) 556-4588 | www.ksma-nc.com
Specializes in teaching self-defense for adults and children.

POLAR ICE HOUSE

Wake Forest

1839 South Main St., Ste. 200
Wake Forest, NC 27587
(919) 453-1500
Youth skating, hockey development, hockey leagues, figure skating and in-line sports for your little cubs.

ACTIVITIES

55

THE BEST DAD/CHILD
STORES

ALL FUN AND GAMES
Apex

958 US Hwy. 64
Apex, NC 27523
(919) 468-6322 | www.allfunngames.com
Carries a great selection of board games, puzzles, brain teasers, collectible and trading cards.

ALI CAT
Carrboro

300 N. Greensboro St.
Carrboro, NC 27510
(919) 932-3954
Specialty toy store with an especially nice selection of puppets. Located in the Carr Mill Mall.

RED HEN
Carrboro

201 Weaver St.
Carrboro, NC 27510
(919) 942-4420 | www.theredhen.com
New and used children's clothing, toys, gifts, books.

ASHWORTH'S
Cary

105 W. Chatham St.
Cary, NC 27511
(919) 467-1877 | www.ashworthdrugs.com
Take a break (from whatever you might be doing in Cary) and pop in to Ashworth's for a vintage soda from the soda fountain.

CAMELOT TREASURES
Cary

251 Grande Heights Dr.
Cary, NC 27513
(919) 388-1708 | www.camelot-treasures.com
Visitors to Camelot Treasures can find costumes, jewelry, home decor, music and more reminiscent of a walk down Harry Potter's Diagon Alley.

DRYER MUSIC STUDIO
Cary

1210 SE Maynard Rd. Ste. 102
Cary, NC 27511
(919) 605-7508 | www.dryermusicstudio.com
Dryer Music Studio offers lessons for children and adults in piano, clarinet, flute, guitar, and violin. Students participate in studio recitals and other performances.

PATTYWHACKS
Cary

1245 Kildaire Farm Rd.
Cary, NC 27511
(919) 468-1928 | www.pattywhacks.com
Pattywhacks is a friendly children's boutique selling fashionable clothes for little ones from infant to size ten (for girls) and size seven (for boys).

PETITE SOLES
Cary

309 Ledgestone Way (Stone Creek Village)
Cary, NC 27519
(919) 466-1141 | www.petitesoles.com
Petite Soles offers the latest trends in footwear for children. The store is divided into fantasy areas for "Pirates" and "Princesses."

RELEVE DANCEWEAR
Cary

280 Meeting St.
Cary, NC 27518
(919) 854-4442 | www.relevedancewear.com
Boutique carries a wide array of apparel for you little gymnast, dancer or cheerleader.

SCIENCE SAFARI
Cary

1255 Kildaire Farm Rd.
Cary, NC 27511
(919) 460-6051 | www.scisafari.com
If a toy has something to do with science or nature, it's sure to be found at Science Safari. The small store is stacked high with chemistry sets, robotics, astronomy kits, and everything your kid needs to get an A+ on the science project.

CAMERON'S
Chapel Hill

201 South Estes Dr. (University Mall)
Chapel Hill, NC 27514
(919) 942-5554 | www.camerons-gallery.com
Since 1977, Cameron's has been an experience, not just a store. Started as a craft gallery, it now offers everything from gold earrings to plastic ants, plus gifts, greeting cards, candles, bath toys, jewelry, handbags, animal-head mounts and other highly entertaining, off-the-wall stuff. Don't miss the shrine room—where nothing is for sale—and its Elvis prayer wall.

CHAPEL HILL COMICS
Chapel Hill

316 W. Franklin St.
Chapel Hill, NC 27516
(919) 967-4439 | www.chapelhillcomics.com
A proudly independent, local bookstore specializing in comics and graphic novels.

59

CHILDREN'S STORE
AND TOY CORNER
Chapel Hill

201 S. Estes Dr.
Chapel Hill, NC 27514
(919) 942-8027
Toys, books, clothes, arts and crafts.

FLYLEAF BOOKS
Chapel Hill

752 MLK, Jr. Blvd.
Chapel Hill, NC 27514
(919) 942-7373 | www.flyleafbooks.com
Find children's books, weekly story times, author events and book clubs at this Chapel Hill independent bookstore.

GOOD EARTH POTTERY & GARDEN
Chapel Hill

1515 Twisted Oak Dr.
Chapel Hill, NC 27516
(919) 918-3848 | www.goodearthpotteryandgarden.com
Choose from more than 20 dipping glazes, 25 under-glazes and five different cone-6 clays to unleash the creative potential and maximize fun. Classes, open teaching studio, workshops and summer camps. Owners have more than 20 years experience in pottery and sculpture.

HARRY'S MARKET AT WHITECROSS
Chapel Hill

3300 Highway 54 W.
Chapel Hill, NC 27516
(919) 932-7025 | www.meetmeatharrys.com
Offers local and area organic produce along with hand-made crafts and other goodies. Harry's Third Monday Market is where local farmers, growers, artisans, performers, business owners and crafters sell, display and perform at the market. Call for details.

THE RECYCLERY
Chapel Hill

108 N. Graham St.
Chapel Hill, NC 27516
(919) 533-9196 | www.recyclery.org
A nonprofit organization that accepts donated bicycles and teaches bicycle repair and maintenance skills to community members while they earn their own bikes.

SUNSHINE COMPANY
Chapel Hill

101 Kildare Rd.
Chapel Hill, NC 27516
(919) 960-3794
Toys, tote bags and baking aprons, among other goods.

ART MACHINE STUDIO
Durham

Golden Belt
807 E. Main St. Bldg. 3-103
Durham, NC 27701
www.artmachinestudios.net
Another of the really cool studios at Golden Belt. My 8-year-old is taking encaustic classes here and loves it!

BICYCLE CHAIN
Durham

639 Broad St.
Durham, NC 27705
(919) 286-2453 | www.thebicyclechain.com
Great bike shop. Fun to hang out and fantasize about the latest Cannondale or Rockhopper (even if you're not in the market). Very knowledgeable staff can answer any question about gear and safety. Six Triangle area locations. Check the website for one near you.

BUILD-A-BEAR WORKSHOP
Durham

The Streets at Southpoint
6910 Fayetteville Rd.
Durham, NC 27713
(919) 544-3300 | www.buildabear.com
A combination toy store and workshop that lets kids create their own stuffed animals, Build-a-Bear offers both drop-in fun and party options for little cuddlers. Bears and other lovable, stuffable creatures.

DOLLY'S
Durham

213 W. Main St.
Durham, NC 27701
(919) 682-1471 | www.dollysvintage.com
Try on some groovy sunglasses or fab wigs at Dolly's, Durham's funky downtown shop for all things glam, recently relocated from Brightleaf Square to center city.

61

LABOURLOVE GALLERY
Durham

Golden Belt
807 E Main St. Ste. 2-130
Durham, NC 27701
(919) 373-4451 | www.labourlove.com

LabourLove sells original artwork, limited edition prints in multiple sizes at affordable prices, clothing, home decor (think pillows and furniture) and other fun and artsy stuff. LabourLove is the most visible anchor in Golden Belt's exciting art district and a leader in the burgeoning art scene in Durham. Come out on Third Fridays for exhibits, fundraisers, music, etc.

MORGAN IMPORTS
Durham

113 S. Gregson St.
Durham, NC 27701
(919) 688-1150 | www.morganimports.com

Huge, two-story gift store includes a dandy toy and children's book section. Bathroom key attached to a tennis racket (guess nobody will be accidently taking that with them) and the Snow Village in the back are both big hits with my girls. This is the first stop (often the last one) when picking out birthday or Christmas presents. From disco balls to Dr. Seuss books to funky, fuzzy beanbag chairs.

OX AND RABBIT SODA AND SUNDRIES
Durham

732 9th St.
Durham, NC 27705
(919) 286-7850

Part funky gift shop, part soda shop. Quite excellent root beer floats and Oreo strawberry milkshakes. Has the feel of a 50's diner but hipper.

PARKER AND OTIS
Durham

112 S. Duke St.
Durham, NC 27701
(919) 683-3200 | www.parkerandotis.com

Gourmet grocery and restaurant featuring locally grown food and beverages, gift shop with plenty of fun and unique kid stuff, including the ever popular (in my household anyway) Boogaloo collection by BlaBla Kids. Lodged in a historic 1904 warehouse, its wares also hark back to the days of penny candy - it has a huge selection of confections (that now cost slightly more than a penny, however). Friday night music on the porch in the summer.

PLAYHOUSE TOYS
Durham

702 9th St.
Durham, NC 27705
(919) 286-1317 | www.playhousetoys.com

A Durham landmark, known for its quality toys, friendly staff and community involvement. Can't decide which game or CD to buy? Borrow it from their lending library and try it first. If you have a kid who loves craft projects, music, trains, stuffed animals or science, they probably have a merchandise club they can join. Call for details.

THE REGULATOR
Durham

720 9th St.
Durham, NC 27705
(919) 286-2700 | www.regulatorbookshop.com

Great gobs of great books. Many a Curious George book has been read on that funky sofa in the children's section by yours truly.

SALSA BABIES AND SALSA TOTS
Durham

3400-A8 Westgate Dr.
Durham, NC 27707
(919) 730-1854 | www.trianglesalsababies.com

Introduces young children to music and movement. Classes, events and parties. Latin and international music. Fiesta!

SHOE CARNIVAL
Durham

North Pointe Shopping Center
1515 North Pointe Dr. Unit #120
Durham, NC 27705
(919) 220-1504 | www.shoecarnival.com

Shoe Carnival stocks footwear for the entire family at reasonable prices. A store emcee announces sales specials and offers customers the opportunity to spin a prize wheel to win in-store discounts. That's good family fun.

STRASBURG CHILDREN
Durham

The Streets at Southpoint
6910 Fayetteville Rd.
Durham, NC 27713
(919) 361-3503 | www.strasburgchildren.com

Ok, if the little ones need to get really dressed up for a wedding or bar mitzvah, this is a good place to go. They've got smocked dresses, christening gowns, communion dresses, and fancy schmanzy suits for boys.

STORES

63

STORES

ULTIMATE COMICS
Durham

756 9th St.
Durham, NC 27705
(919) 286-0410 | www.ultimatecomicsonline.com
Great collection of comic books for kids.

JOYFUL SOUNDS ACADEMY OF MUSIC AND ART
Fuquay-Varina

117 E. Vance St.
Fuquay-Varina, NC 27526
(919) 552-8219 | www.joyfulsoundsacademy.com
Instruction in piano, voice, violin, guitar, banjo, mandolin, dulcimer, brass, percussion, art and more.... by accomplished and degreed instructions. Private lessons or small group classes.

GAME STOP
Garner

171 Shenstone Ln.
Garner, NC 27529
(919) 733-1276 | www.gamestop.com
The place to tend to your Xbox and Playstation needs. Several locations throughout the Triangle.

PURPLE CROW BOOKS
Hillsborough

109 W. King St.
Hillsborough, NC 27278
(919) 732-1711 | www.purplecrowbooks.com
The Children's Room at this popular Hillsborough bookseller is a place where kids can go to explore the world. Visit the website to learn about upcoming events for kids.

TOY FACTORY
Hillsborough

110 Boone Sq. #19
Hillsborough, NC 27278
(919) 732-2155 | www.thetoyfactory.com
Offering toys, arts and crafts and hobby supplies, this Hillsborough landmark also hosts weekly in-store gaming tournaments.

PITTSBORO TOYS
Pittsboro

44B Hillsboro St.
Pittsboro, NC 27312
(919) 542-4885 | www.pittsborotoys.com
Local handmade toys and well-known brands like LEGO and Grund. The place in Pittsboro to get your Webkinz fix.

311 WEST MAIN STREET
GALLERIES AND STUDIOS   Raleigh

311 W. Main St.
Raleigh, NC 27601
(919) 821-2262 | www.311galleriesandstudios.org
Located in the Warehouse District of Raleigh. There are currently 14 tenant artists working and showing in the studios and galleries of 311. The exhibition space features the work of tenant artists and emerging artists as well as some of Raleigh's favorite established artists.

ANIMAL QUACKERS TOY STORE   Raleigh

13200 Strickland Rd.
Raleigh, NC 27613
(919) 844-9771
Retro toys and the hottest new items for kids make for a swell time for dads and kids alike.

BARNES & NOBLE   Raleigh

4325 Glenwood Ave.
Raleigh, NC 27612
(919) 782-0030 | www.barnesandnoble.com
You'll always find a great selection of books and videos, many discounted, and incredible savings on clearance items. Plus, a fine children's book section to relax and read together for a while.

BEEHIVE STUDIOS   Raleigh

107 W. Hargett St. (3rd Floor of Father & Son Antiques)
(919) 832-3030
Gallery and seven artist studios supporting new, locally grown art and live music monthly.

BE TWEEN   Raleigh

530 Daniels St.
Raleigh, NC 27605
(919) 839-0061
A children's clothing store that strives to keep those picky 'tweens happy. But it's not limited to soon-to-be teenagers, the boutique has something for everyone, from babies up to size 16.

BORDERS
Raleigh

8825 N. Six Forks Rd.
Raleigh, NC 27615
(919) 845-1154 | www.borders.com
Border's carries books, videos, and CDs with many discounted items. The store offers a few cozy places to curl up with a book and a great kids' section. Several other locations throughout the Triangle, as well.

THE CARTER BUILDING STUDIOS
Raleigh

12-22 Glenwood Ave
Raleigh, NC 27603
www.thecarterbuilding.com
A collection of art studios featuring up to 80+ working artisans and their work.

CATHY'S PAINT YOUR OWN
Raleigh

8111-147 Creedmore Rd.
Raleigh, NC 27613
(919) 976-0220 | www.cathyspaintyourown.com
A fun atmosphere to paint a masterpiece for grandpa. They'll host school groups and camps, but walk-ins are always welcome.

CHILDREN'S ORCHARD
Raleigh

2865 Jones Franklin Rd.
Raleigh, NC 27606
(919) 852-0050 | www.childrensorchard.com
A resale/retail boutique that features brand-name, top quality, gently used and new kid's clothing, toys, furniture, equipment, books, and accessories.

DILLY DALLY AT OH BABY!
Raleigh

4209 Lassiter Mill Rd.
Raleigh, NC 27609
(919) 844-7557 | www.dillydallystores.com
Local, family-owned children's clothing and furniture boutique. Store named after the owner's grandmother, Mama Dillie.

THE DISNEY STORE
Raleigh

4325 Glenwood Ave.
Raleigh, NC 27612
(919) 571-1844 | www.disneystore.com
It's a small world after all, but parents may feel like they followed Alice down the rabbit hole when they cross the threshold of a Disney Store. For kids, it might seem more like nirvana.

FAO SCHWARZ AT MACY'S

Raleigh

4325 Glenwood Ave.
Raleigh, NC 27612
(800) 426-8697 | www.foa.com
The quintessential toy store... a little piece of Manhattan in Brier Creek.

JERRY'S ARTORAMA

Raleigh

3060 Wake Forest Rd.
Raleigh, NC 27609
(919) 876-6610 | www.raleigh.jerrysartaramastores.com
The go-to place for art supplies at great prices. Ask any artist in the Triangle and that's what you'll hear. Offers one-day art workshops for kids throughout the year.

JJ'S KIDS CUTS

Raleigh

6136 Falls of the Neuse Rd.
Raleigh, NC 27609
(919) 873-1600 | www.jjskidscuts.com
Is your mop-topped kid a little squirrelly about getting his or her hair cut? JJ's is the antidote. Cuts and styles for children of all ages in a very kid-friendly environment, including a giant climbing structure and TVs and videos at each station.

LEARNING EXPRESS

Raleigh

4151 Main At North Hills Ste.110
Raleigh, NC 27609
(919) 881-4141 | www.learningexpress.com
The first Learning Express store was opened to help fund a pre-school in Massachusetts, and the chain has grown to become the nation's largest franchiser of specialty toy stores.

LEGO STORE

Raleigh

4325 Glenwood Ave.
Raleigh, NC 27612
(919) 787-5771
www.stores.lego.com/en-us/Raleigh/LandingPage.aspx
Don't plan on zipping quickly in and out of this store, which features plenty of play tables and piles of LEGO blocks for inspired building.

MOBLEY'S CHILDREN'S SHOES

Raleigh

7416 Creedmoor Rd.
Raleigh, NC 27615
(919) 518-1640 | www.mobleyshoes.com
Triangle-dwellers will tell you: Mobley's is where you take the little ones to buy shoes. No frills, just dependable kids' shoes.

MOXIE KIDS
Raleigh

2026 Cameron St.
Raleigh, NC 27605
(919) 821-3341 | www.moxiekidsonline.com
Hip clothes for the under-8 crowd.

NICK'S TRAINS, INC.
Raleigh

5201 Oak Park Rd.
Raleigh, NC 27612
www.nicks-trains.com
New and used toy and model trains for the aspiring conductor.

ORNAMENTEA
Raleigh

509 N. West St.
Raleigh, NC 27603
(919) 834-6260 | www.ornamentea.com
Breakfast treats and coffee served 8:30-10 am on Fridays. Children enjoy art projects and books while parents socialize. Yes, there's likely to be more moms than dads, but hey, who can turn down free coffee and treats?

PB&J FUN FACTORY
Raleigh

5901 Fayetteville Rd.
Raleigh, NC 27603
(919) 661-2738 | www.arcadegames4u.com
A specialty home game room store that specializes in billiard tables, arcade games, pinball machines and many other gameroom items—including toys.

QUAIL RIDGE BOOKS
Raleigh

3522 Wade Ave
Raleigh, NC 27607-4048
(919) 828-1588 | www.quailridgebooks.com
Open 9 to 9 daily, specializes in fine literature for adults and kids, with a special focus on the south. They have a well-earned reputation for supporting local writers.

SHUTTERBUGS
Raleigh

619 Oberlin Rd.
Raleigh, NC 27605
(919) 833-7527 | www.shutterbugsboutique.com
Children's clothing and gifts... casual wear such as pajamas and winter coats as well as formal wear for your little flower girl or ring bearer.

STORYBOOK SAFARI
Raleigh

8320 Litchford Rd. Ste. 134
Raleigh, NC
(919) 876-5466 | www.storybooksafari.com

Billed as "The Learning Center for Kids," Storybook Safari uses art, music, and games to help pre-school and elementary-age children develop reading skills in conjunction with a love of education and books.

THE TEACH ME STORE
Raleigh

3520 Spring Forest Rd.
Raleigh, NC 27616
(919) 872-2747 | www.teachmestore.com

The Teach Me Store offers a wide variety of toys, books, crafts, and educational supplies. Their large inventory includes software, electronic games, puppets and science kits galore.

TOYS R US
Raleigh

4325 Glenwood Ave.
Raleigh, NC 27612
(919) 787-2121 | www.toysrus.com

Who doesn't love Geoffrey? Plus, the original toy superstore chain has a nice selection of Radio Flyer products.

WJ'S TOY STOP
Raleigh

14460 New Falls of Neuse Rd. # 165
Raleigh, NC 27614
(919) 453-2869

Specializes in unique, hard-to-find toys...courteous and helpful staff.

ZANY BRAINY
Raleigh

6250 Glenwood Ave.
Raleigh, NC 27614
(919) 781-6255 | www.zanybrainy.com

Guided by the principle that kids learn best while having fun... store stocks tons of educational toys, phonics laptops, numbers and counting activity sets, colorform maps... for your future Mensa members.

LOLLIPOP TOY SHOP
Wake Forest

1839 Main St., Ste. 140
Wake Forest, NC 27587
(919) 453-2393 | www.thelollipoptoyshop.com

Traditional toy store featuring dolls, strollers, stuffed animals, scientific toys, games, puzzles, stickers, nickel candy...

STORYTELLER'S BOOKSTORE
Wake Forest

100 Roosevelt Ave.
Wake Forest, NC 27587
(919) 554-9146 | www.storystorewf.com

Storytelling performances, readings by authors and workshops for children and adults. The store is furnished with a grand piano and a red leather antique barber chair, aka the "storyteller's chair." Paintings and photography from local artists adorn the wall.

TOADS AND TULIPS
Wake Forest

306 S. White St.
Wake Forest, NC 27587
(919) 562-9299 | www.toadsandtulips.com

Located in historic Wake Forest inside the Cotton Company; offers toys, baby gear and furniture. If you can't make it out to Wake Forest, they also have an impressive on-line retail store on their website.

THE BEST DAD/CHILD
OUTDOOR PARKS & RECREATION

OUTDOOR PARKS

GREEN LEVEL GOURD FARM   Apex
3800 Green Level Rd. West
Apex, NC 27523
(919) 387-7352 | www.greenlevelgourdfarm.com
Interested in gourds? This is the place for you. The gift shop features gourd baskets, bowls, jewelry, dolls, bird houses and Christmas ornaments. Gourd birdhouse craft classes are offered upon request for $10 per person. Five generations of the Hubert Lewter family have lived on the farm for nearly a century.

JEAN'S BERRY PATCH   Apex
3003 NC Hwy 751
Apex, NC 27523
www.jeansberrypatch.com
Nothing could be finer than picking strawberries in Carolina in the Springtime at Jean's.

JORDAN LAKE   Apex
280 State Park Rd.
Apex, NC 27523
www.ncparks.gov/visit/parks/jord/main.php
Fishing, hiking, picnicking, swimming, boating, camping... nearly 50,000 acres. An adequate substitute when the kids are begging to go to the beach but you're just not up for the 2-hr trek to Wrightsville.

CARRBORO FARMER'S MARKET   Carrboro
301 W. Main St.
Carrboro, NC 27510
(919) 280-3326 | www.carrborofarmersmarket.com
Saturdays 7 AM – Noon, Wednesdays 3:30 PM – 6:30 PM; Spring, Summer, Fall... Get your veggies then climb trees at the lawn at Weaver St. Market...a perfect Saturday morning in Carrboro.

UNIVERSITY LAKE   Carrboro
Jones Ferry Rd.
Carborro, NC
(919) 942-8007 | www.carrboro.com/universitylake.html
Canoe and boat rentals, fishing and picnicking. The lake is open between late March and early November.

FRED G. BOND METRO PARK   Cary
801 High House Rd.
Cary, NC 27512
At 310 acres, Fred G. Bond Metro Park is one of the largest municipal parks in Wake County. Picnic areas, athletic fields, walking trails, the Lazy Daze Playground and the Sertoma Amphitheatre.

GREEN ACRES
Cary

1132 Morrisville Carpenter Rd.
Cary, NC 27519
www.greenacrescary.com
Green Acres is the place to be... for corn mazes and pumpkins in the fall and Christmas trees in the winter.

HEMLOCK BLUFFS
NATURE PRESERVE
Cary

2616 Kildare Farm Rd.
Cary, NC 27513
(919) 387-5980 | www.hemlockbluffs.org
Go bird-watching among strands of hemlock trees. Observation decks, hiking trails, picnic areas.

KOKA BOOTH AMPHITHEATER
Cary

8003 Regency Pky.,
Cary, NC 27518
(919) 462-2025 | www.boothampitheater.com
Nestled amongst the tall hardwoods and pines that grow alongside Symphony Lake, the Koka Booth Amphitheater offers a stunning spot for a concert, festival, and 4th of July fireworks show.

STEVENS NATURE CENTER
Cary

2616 Kildaire Farm Rd.
Cary, NC 27518
(919) 387-5980 | www.townofcary.org
Located at Hemlock Bluffs Nature Preserve, a 3,700-foot facility containing an exhibit hall and classroom space, as well as an outdoor education shelter.

BOOTHILL FARM
Chapel Hill

2618 Orange Chapel Garden Glover Rd.
Chapel Hill, NC 27516
(919) 967-2994
Spend a day riding horses on the miles of trails at this 100-year-old family farm. Take riding and jumping lessons.

GENESIS FARM
Chapel Hill

1841 Jo Mac Rd.
Chapel Hill, NC 27526
(919) 968-4759 | www.genesisfarm.com
Farm tour includes a visit to the barnyard and gardens where you can purchase eggs and veggies. Summer camps available.

75

JOHNSTON MILL
NATURE PRESERVE
Chapel Hill

Mount Sinai Rd. (off NC Hwy. 86)
Chapel Hill, NC 27514
(919) 833-3662

Located 1.1 miles east of NC Highway 86, with a parking area on the right just before New Hope Creek. Three miles of intimate hiking trails traverse this 296-acre sanctuary. Explore mature forests, discover historic mill sites and splash in bubbling creeks. Enjoy the wonders of nature just minutes from downtown Chapel Hill.

MEADOWMONT SWIM CLUB
Chapel Hill

301 Old Barn Lane
Chapel Hill, NC 27517
(919) 945-0650 | www.meadowmontclub.com

Annual and seasonal memberships available; or swim for the day. Includes a regulation size lap pool; fun pool with a 98-foot water slide, raindrop and shoreline entry; band shell within the pool deck for entertaining; children's playground; park gazebo; sand volleyball court; basketball goal; a clubhouse with snack bar and kitchen for catered events, and more. Year-round activities for various ages, including themed summer-camp programs. Birthday party options are also available.

NC BOTANICAL GARDENS
Chapel Hill

Totten Center
US 15-501/ NC Hwy 54 Bypass
Chapel Hill, NC 27514
(919) 962-0522 | www.ncbg.unc.edu

Look for fairies hidden in the herb garden, dig in the dirt with giant shovels and giant tic-tac-toe blocks or play in the natural tree house.

SPENCE'S FARM FOR KIDS
Chapel Hill

6407 Mill House Rd
Chapel Hill, NC 27516
(919) 968-8581 | www.spencesfarm.com

Summer camps, afterschool program, mini camps during school year holidays. A wonderful place for children to learn about farm life, animals, organic gardening, hiking, outdoor adventuring and more!

AL BUEHLER TRAIL
AT DUKE UNIVERSITY   Durham

NC Hwy 751 and Science Dr.
Durham, NC 27705
(919) 613-8013
More than three miles of gravel jogging and walking trails among the forest around Washington Duke Inn. Named for Al Buehler, former Duke track coach and six-time ACC champion.

CENTRAL PARK   Durham

534 Foster St.
Durham, NC 27701
(919) 794-8194 | www.durhamcentralpark.org
At the heart of what is evolving into a cool, family-friendly part of town, Central Park is home to tons of festivals and gatherings as well as the downtown Farmer's Market, Skate Park (mostly a teen hangout and can be a little dangerous for little ones I recently discovered), and gigantic metal turtle and bird sculptures that kids love to climb on.

DUKE FOREST   Durham

Duke University West Campus
Durham, NC 27705
(919) 613-8013 | www.nicholas.duke.edu/forest
7,600 acre teaching and research forest of Duke University, with a variety of ecosystems represented. Great place to escape and hike, bike, ride horses, fish and picnic.

DUKE GARDENS   Durham

426 Anderson St.
Durham, NC 27705
(919) 684-3698 | www.hr.duke.edu/dukegardens
Surely everyone who lives in the area has visited Duke Gardens, whether or not you have children. Parents swoon at the acres of roses and other impeccably presented flowers and plants, spread out over 55 acres. Kids love the wide open spaces and steep hills for rolling down. Bring plenty of bread for the ducks and geese but don't be surprised if the suddenly ap-pearing- out -of -nowhere catfish get to it first. Attracts more than 300,000 visitors from around the world each year. On campus at Duke University.

DUKE PARK   Durham

106 W. Knox St.
Durham, NC 27701
(919) 560-4355 | www.durhamnc.gov/departments/parks
May be THE most popular park in Durham. It's huge. If it's good weather, count on there being hordes of laughing, screaming children.

77

OUTDOOR PARKS

ENO RIVER
Durham

4404 Guess Rd.
Durham, NC 27712
www.enoriver.org

Truly one of the great things about this area, the Eno is a beautiful, meandering river with plenty of fun activities in and alongside it: swimming, fishing, rock-skipping, hiking trails and bluffs to explore.

FORREST HILLS PARK
Durham

1639 University Dr.
Durham, NC 27707
(919) 560-4782 | www.durhamnc.gov/departments/parks

One of the larger parks in Durham, the water feature is a very popular hangout on hot summer days, especially considering most of the play area is shade-less. Experienced park goers bring a swim suit or a change of clothes. Note: my daughters made a killing selling lemonade here one particularly hot summer day.

GANYARD HILL FARM
Durham

319 Sherron Rd.
Durham, NC 27703
(919) 596-8728 | www.pumpkincountry.com

Pumpkin patch, cornfield mazes, giant haystack, hayrides, complimentary pumpkins, bees; drop in (no reservation required).

HERNDON HILLS FARM
Durham

7110 Massey Chapel Rd.
Durham, NC 27713

Pick your own blueberries, blackberries or muscadines. Who would have ever thought that such a beautiful farm, which has been in the Herndon family since the 1700's, would be tucked away so close to Southpoint mall?

LAKE MICHIE
Durham

2303 Bahama Rd.
Durham, NC 27503
(919) 477-3906 | www.durhamnc.gov/departments/parks/lakemichie

Lake Michie offers visitors a place to fish, boat, hike, and picnic. Boats and motors are available for rent.

LITTLE RIVER PARK
Durham

301 Little River Way (off Guess Rd.)
Durham, NC 27572
(919) 245-2660 | www.enoriver.org/eno/parks/littleriverpark.html
Seven miles of hiking trails and eight miles of mountain bike trails and a smooth paved path for new bikers (part of the Eno River Park). Park straddles the Orange and Durham County line. Frog Frenzy, Tiny Trekkers, Birds for Beginners, Monarch Migration, Fossil Find; there is lots of fun stuff for little explorers to discover.

LEIGH FARM PARK
Durham

370 Leigh Farm Rd.
Durham, NC 27707
(919) 560-4355
90-acre nature preserve is home to the Piedmont Wildlife Center.

NEW HOPE BOTTOMLANDS TRAIL
Durham

4800 Chapel Hill Rd.
Durham, NC 27707
(919) 560-4355
2.2 mile walking trail through the New Hope Creek flood plain. Trail begins near Githens Middle School.

NORTHGATE PARK
Durham

300 W. Club Blvd.
Durham, NC 277
(919) 560-4355 | www.durhamnc.gov/departments/parks
Across the street from Club Boulevard Elementary School, this is another one of those under-utilized parks in Durham. The play area is unique. The main structure is more of a fitness center than a play structure. The slide has no sides (little ones will need a little help).The climbing structure is made of rope and resembles a spider web; consequently the park has long been referred to as "Spider Park" by my daughters. There are plenty of gazebos and seating areas for picnics and birthday parties.

ORCHARD PARK
Durham

1000 S. Duke St
Durham, NC 27707
(919) 460.9596 | www.durhamnc.gov/departments/parks
Perhaps the best kept secret in Durham. Located just south of downtown, this park offers wide open green spaces perfect for flying kites, tossing Frisbees or playing freeze tag. It has the obligatory swings and slides and sand boxes but it also has an interesting stone maze structure that seems to fascinate young kids, plus a community garden (hopefully, the community doesn't mind if a cute 4-year-old samples the tomatoes every now and then).

79

TRINITY PARK   Durham
410 Watts St.
Durham, NC 27701
(919) 560-4355 | www.durhamnc.gov/departments/parks
A small park tucked away in the Trinity Park neighborhood, it's a perfect way to swing away an afternoon with your pre-schooler. Popular hangout for the 5-and-under crowd, although older kids may get bored.

TRITON STABLES   Durham
2521 Baptist Rd.
Durham, NC 27703
(919) 957-1931 | www.tritonstables.net
Group and private lessons for beginning to advanced riders, as well as competition training. Triton also offers annual summer camps for young riders.

RAFTING THE ENO   Durham
5101 N. Roxboro Rd.
Durham, NC 27712
(919) 471-3802
Two-hour natural history float trips on the Eno River, led by naturalist, "River Dave" Owen. River Dave has been guiding tours of the Eno River for fifteen years! He also knows everything there is to know about trees. All ages; call for reservations. Trips from April through September. Tours depart from West Point on the Eno Park, Monday–Saturday, at 10 am and 3 pm. Owen also offers evening wafting around the time of each full moon.

WALLER FAMILY FARM   Durham
5030 Kerley Rd.
Durham, NC 27705
(919) 225-4305 | www.wallerfamilyfarm.com
Pick your own strawberries while you hear the cows bellow from the nearby meadow.

SUNSET RIDGE RACQUET
AND SWIM CLUB   Holly Springs
5032 Linksland Dr.
Holly Springs, NC 27540
(919) 557-0000 | www.sunsetridge.com
Swim and tennis lessons plus summer sports camps are available at this neighborhood retreat.

HARPER PARK   Knightdale

207 Main St.
Knightdale, NC 27545
(919) 217-2230
Harper Park features five picnic areas with grills, a gazebo and a children's play area.

LAKE CRABTREE COUNTY PARK   Morrisville

1400 Aviation Pkwy.
Morrisville, NC 27560
(919) 460-3390
215-acre park located on the shores of a scenic 520-acre flood control lake; offers hiking, cycling, nature trails, boat rentals, two children's playgrounds, playing fields, picnic facilities and environmental education programs.

BLUE JAY POINT COUNTY PARK   Raleigh

3200 Pleasant Union Church Rd.
Raleigh, NC 27614
(919) 870-4330 | www.wakegov.com/parks/bluejay
Its 236 acres border Falls Lake, and its natural setting is conducive to outdoor activities and environmental education.

DURANT NATURE PARK   Raleigh

8305 Camp Durant Rd.
Raleigh, NC 27614
(919) 870-2871
The heavily forested park, covering 237 acres, offers five miles of hiking trails, scenic overlooks, two lakes, wildflower and fern gardens.

E. CARROLL JOYNER PARK   Raleigh

701 Harris Rd.
Wake Forest, NC 27587
www.wakeforestnc.gov
117 acres, farm buildings, pecan groves, amphitheater, three miles of walking trails, great for rollerblading or biking.

OUTDOOR PARKS

HISTORIC YATES MILL COUNTY PARK

Raleigh

4620 Lake Wheeler Rd.
Raleigh, NC 27603
(919) 856-6675 | www.wakegov.com/parks/yatesmill

The centerpiece of Yates Mill Park is the grist mill that gives the park its name. The mill is the only remaining mill of its type in Wake County and is fully restored and operational.

LAKE WHEELER PARK

Raleigh

6404 Lake Wheeler Rd.
Raleigh, NC 27603
(919) 662-5704

150 acres of parkland and a 650-acre lakes means fishing, sailing, canoeing, rowing, kayaking, sand volleyball and picnicking abound.

LAUREL HILLS PARK AND RECREATIONAL CENTER

Raleigh

3808 Edwards Mill Rd.
Raleigh NC 27612
(919) 831-6856

Home to the popular and innovative All Children's Playground, designed for the use and enjoyment of children of all physical capabilities. The playground has a wooden play structure of tunnels, bridges, towers, swings, and rings built over soft sand. The park also includes a community center, lighted ball fields, outdoor basketball courts, and a pond.

MOORE SQUARE

Raleigh

200 S. Blount St.
Raleigh, NC 27601
(919) 832-1231 | www.godowntownraleigh.com/go/moore-square

In addition to hosting an outdoor film series during the summer months, Moore Square is home to Raleigh's iconic acorn sculpture, designed by artist David Benson to commemorate the city's bicentennial.

MUSEUM PARK

Raleigh

2110 Blue Ridge Rd.
Raleigh, NC 27607
(919) 839-6262 | www.ncartmuseum.org/museum_park/visit_park

The Museum Park consists of 164 acres of woodlands, open areas and streams filled with trails and monumental works of environmental art. The combination of an important art museum and a large natural area offers a rare opportunity to explore art and ecology together.

PRAIRIE RIDGE ECO-STATION   Raleigh
4301 Reedy Creek Rd.
Raleigh, NC 27607
(919) 733-7450 | www.naturalsciences.org/prairie-ridge-ecostation
A division of the NC Museum of Natural Sciences, established for research and educational purposes, the eco-station is 45 acres of Piedmont prairie, forests, ponds, a stream and sustainable buildings featuring integrated wildlife friendly landscape. Two walking trails open to the public.

PULLEN PARK   Raleigh
520 Ashe Ave.
Raleigh, NC 27606
(919) 831-6468 | www.raleighfree.com/pullen_park.html
Pullen Park's best known attraction is the 1921 Dentzel carousel. Featuring more than 50 hand carved and hand painted animals, it was accepted into the National Register of Historic Places in 1976. Some of the animals move, some are stationary. In addition to 30 horses, other animals on the carousel include ostriches, rabbits, cats, pigs, a tiger, a goat, and a lion. The cost to ride it is $1, which is way worth the very long, fun musical ride that ensues! Also features a snack bar, large playgrounds, paved walking trails, indoor Olympic-size swimming pool open year-round, a 1950's miniature train ride ($1), and a kiddie boat ride ($1).

SHELLEY LAKE   Raleigh
1400 E. Millbrook Rd.
Raleigh, NC 27609
(919) 420-2331
50-acre lake offers kids and their dads a wide variety of recreational opportunities; fishing, canoeing, sailing, row boating, pedal boating, hiking and picnicking.

SILVER LAKE WATERPARK   Raleigh
5300 Tryon Rd.
Raleigh, NC 27606
(919) 851-1683 | www.sssrc.org
Shallow kiddie area, "The Beast" waterslide, bumper boats, sea monster, test your skills on the water log (aka try not to embarrass yourself on the water log), playground, horseshoes, pedal boats. Open daily in the summer and weekends the rest of the year (weather permitting).

THEATRE IN THE PARK   Raleigh
107 Pullen Rd.
Raleigh, NC 27606
(919) 831-6058 | www.theatreinthepark.com
Located in the northern end of Raleigh's scenic Pullen Park and internationally acclaimed for its outstanding theatrical achievements, Theatre in the Park is the largest community theater in North Carolina.

83

OUTDOOR PARKS

WILLIAM UMSTEAD PARK   Raleigh

8801 Glenwood Ave
Raleigh, NC 27617,
(919) 571 4170 | www.stateparks.com/william_b_umstead.html
With three man-made lakes and a forest, it's easy to spend an entire day in this quiet oasis tucked between Raleigh, Cary and Durham. 22 miles of hiking trails. Rent canoes and rowboats to explore the lakes.

THE BEST DAD/CHILD
UNIQUE ADVENTURES

NC ZOO
Asheboro

4403 Zoo Pkwy.
Asheboro, NC 27205
(800) 488-0444 | www.nczoo.org

The North Carolina Zoo has so much to offer and is worth the drive! Plan lots of time to visit, as the Zoo is quite large. In fact, our zoo is the nation's largest walk-through zoo, featuring more than 500 acres of walkways and more than 1,100 animals. The NC Zoo has separate North America, Australia, and Africa sections, each of which could be a separate day trip. Dress appropriately for the weather and wear comfortable walking shoes. Bring sunscreen and binoculars, and of course, don't forget your camera!

CARRBORO SUNDAY ARTS AND CRAFTS MARKET
Carrboro

301 W. Main St.
Carrboro, NC 27510
(919) 929-3986

2nd and 4th Sunday of each month, April – December, 1 PM – 5 PM. Make stuff or buy stuff.

WEAVER STREET MARKET
Carrboro

301 Weaver St.
Carrboro, NC 27510
www.weaverstreetmarket.coop/

Live open air music on Sundays. Choose from the Market's many buffet selections and have brunch outside at the picnic tables or on a blanket while you enjoy the music, impromptu dancing and hula-hooping. Stop by the Market for some wonderful organic groceries and fresh produce while you are there!

DADDY-DAUGHTER DANCE
Cary

120 Maury O'Dell Pl.
Cary, NC 27512
(919) 462-3970

This annual father-daughter dance is sure to make your daughter's first dance a memorable one. Open to girls ages 4 through 12. Cost is $17 per person if you live in Cary or $22 per person if you don't. The dance is held at the Cary Senior Center, usually around Valentine's Day. Call for details.

KITE FESTIVAL   Cary

801 High House Rd.
Cary, NC 27512
(919) 469-4100

Fun, day-long event held at Cary's Bond Park each spring. Expert kite flyers on hand for stunt kite demos, special awards and certificates in a variety of kite flying categories, such as best crash, smallest kite, largest tail, youngest flyer, most unique kite, best home-made kite. FUN!

SPRING DAZE ARTS AND CRAFTS FESTIVAL   Cary

801 High House Rd.
Cary, NC 27512
(919) 469-4100

Celebrate Spring at the annual Cary art event, held each year in the 310-acre Fred G. Bond Metro Park, a perfect setting with its winding trails, a lush forested canopy, and a beautiful lake. The festival is filled arts and crafts, your favorite festival foods, community based civic groups handing out information on things you can get involved with, and entertainment. Children will be delighted by activities just for them in the Children's Village and will be invited to exercise their imagination as they play in the always popular Lazy Daze Playground – the center of the village.

STARLIGHT CONCERTS SERIES   Cary

119 Ambassador Loop
Cary, NC 27512

Bring a lawn chair or blanket and relax under the stars listen to great music! The Starlight Concert Series is a series of free concerts held on Fridays throughout the summer. From reggae to bluegrass to jazz, the series showcases an eclectic mix of local and regional talent. All concerts begin at 7:30 pm in the Page-Walker Arts & History Center Garden.

MOREHEAD PLANETARIUM   Chapel Hill

UNC
250 E. Franklin St.
Chapel Hill, NC
(919) 962-1236 | www.moreheadplanetarium.org

The Morehead Planetarium in downtown Chapel Hill offers numerous planetarium shows and exhibits for children and adults. The Planetarium's "Magic Tree House® Space Mission" show is great for kids 5-12 and dads. This is the first planetarium on a college campus in the U.S. Morehead Planetarium is proud for its work training astronauts for NASA. Its GlaxoSmithKline Fulldome Theater is the largest fulldome digital video planetarium on a college campus in the world.

CAROLINA PANTHERS
Charlotte

800 South Mint St.
Charlotte, NC 28202
(704) 358-7000 | www.panthers.com
The NFL Panthers are only a couple hours from the Triangle and definitely worth a Sunday drive.

CHARLOTTE BOBCATS
Charlotte

333 East Trade St.
Charlotte, NC 28202
(704) 688-8600 | www.nba.com/bobcats
One of the newer NBA franchises, the exciting Bobcats are a fun, young team to watch. Good odds of getting a glimpse of basketball legend Michael Jordan, who is a part owner of the team and often in attendance at home games.

DISCOVERY PLACE
Charlotte

301 N. Tryon St.
Charlotte, NC 28202
(704) 372-6261 | www.discoveryplace.org
One of the leading hands-on science centers in the country, located in the heart of downtown Charlotte.

NASCAR HALL OF FAME
Charlotte

333 East Trade St.
Charlotte, NC 28202
(704) 654-4400 | www.nascarhall.com
No place is car racing bigger than in North Carolina. Experience everything NASCAR at the 150,000 square foot museum in downtown Charlotte.

CEDAR GROVE BLUEBERRY FARM
Cedar Grove

8411 NC Hwy 86 N.
Cedar Grove, NC 27231
(919) 732-1330
Pick-Your-Own Blueberry Farm. Family-owned farm located in rural, northern Orange County. Several picnic tables, as well as a couple of good shade trees to relax under. So, bring a picnic lunch and spend the afternoon with us. Swing set and play area for the kids...not to mention...a lot of naturally grown BLUEBERRIES! Approximately 30 miles north of Chapel Hill. Open during blueberry season dawn until dusk 7-days a week.

AMERICAN DANCE FESTIVAL
Durham

715 Broad St.
Durham, NC 27705
(919) 684-6402 | www.americandancefestival.org

The largest and most influential modern dance festival in the world, featuring more than two dozen modern dance companies and hundreds of choreographers, writers and students participating in classes, seminars and performances for several weeks each summer. Performances are held at various locations throughout Duke University.

BENNETT PLACE
Durham

4409 Bennett Memorial Rd.
Durham, NC 27705
(919) 383-4345 | www.nchistoricsites.org/bennett/bennett.htm

In 1865, Confederate General Johnson and Union General Sherman met here and signed surrender papers for the Southern Armies. Today, the reconstructed farmhouse gives visitors a glimpse into the lifestyle of an ordinary Southern farmer during the Civil War era (you may have to explain to your child, as I did mine, that this was even before you were born).

BIKE TO SCHOOL
Durham

www.durhamnc.gov/departments/transportation/bike_hike_map.cfm

A great way to spend time and have fun with your kid. Check out Durham's new bike and hike map to find safe and fun trails.

CAMERON INDOOR STADIUM
Durham

301 Whiford Dr. (Duke Campus)
Durham, NC 27706
www.goduke.com

Visit the notorious home court for the Duke Blue Devils basketball team and the infamous Cameron Crazies. Men's conference games are a tough ticket but there are usually some floating around for the earlier non-conference games. As the father of little girls, it's important for me to take in women's games to reinforce that they're just as tough as the guys, even though they won't see them on TV as often. The Lady Devils are usually highly ranked nationally too. Don't forget to paint your face blue and go crazy!

CENTERFEST
Durham

Foster St. at Durham Central Park
Durham, NC 27701
(919) 560-2722 | www.centerfest.durhamarts.org

The longest running street arts festival in NC. The streets of downtown Durham come alive with arts, entertainment, food and fun; the two-day festival is usually held during a weekend in September each year.

DUKE CHAPEL
Durham

401 Chapel Dr.
Durham, NC 27708
(919) 884-2921 | www.chapel.duke.edu

Stunningly beautiful, world famous neo-gothic chapel on the highest ridge on Duke's campus, has a 5,600 pipe organ and 50-bell carillon, which can be heard ding-donging throughout campus. Check the website for performances by the Duke Chorale (always a fun treat during the holidays).

DURHAM ART WALK
Durham

120 Morris St.
Durham, NC 27701
(919) 560-ARTS | www.durhamartwalk.com

Held twice a year, in the Spring and Fall, the Art Walk sprawls from the Durham Arts Council throughout downtown. The two-day event typically features over 200 artists and dozens of downtown venues plus music, food and fun activities.

DURHAM CHAMBER OF COMMERCE
Durham

300 W. Morgan St. #1400
Durham, NC 27701
(919) 682-2133 | www.durhamchamber.org

Find your house from the breathtaking view of Durham and beyond from the 14th floor Durham Chamber window of the 15-story blue glass building downtown.

DURHAM PERFORMING ARTS CENTER
Durham

123 Vivian St.
Durham, NC 27701
(919) 680-2787 | www.dpacnc.com

One of downtown Durham's latest additions, the magnificent, state-of-the art center hosts an impressive lineup of music concerts and Broadway productions, many suitable for children, such as stage productions of The Lion King, Madagascar, Shrek the Musical, and Disney's Imagination Movers in 2011. Check the website for performances being added.

FESTIVAL FOR THE ENO   Durham

West Point on the Eno
5101 N. Roxboro St.
Durham, NC 27712
www.enoriver.org/Festival
The annual 3-day fundraising event takes place around the 4th of July each year. The festival is all about music, art, community and raising money for and awareness about the Eno. The festival usually lands some popular, national musical acts. Definitely worth exploring, whether you're a music or river lover.

GREAT HUMAN RACE   Durham

Annual event in Downtown Durham
www.greathumanrace.org
5k walk and run raises thousands of dollars for dozens of local nonprofit organizations; lots of festivities on the day of the race, usually held in early Spring, course winds through downtown Durham; great way to teach your kid the value of giving back to the community, while having fun and getting some exercise together at the same time. Sponsored by the Volunteer Center of Durham (www.thevolunteercenter.org).

WALLTOWN CHILDREN'S THEATRE   Durham

1225 Berkeley Street
Durham, NC 27705
(919) 286-4545 | www.walltownchildrenstheatre.org
Summer camp sessions from June to July, 9 am to 3 pm. These are award-winning camps (profiled on CNN News, Public Television and featured at the Kennedy Center for Performing Arts and the Rock and Roll Hall of Fame). Be sure to check the website for upcoming performances.

WET AND WILD EMERALD POINTE   Greensboro

3910 South Holden Rd.
Greensboro, NC 27406
(336) 852-9721| www.emeraldpointe.com
Large water park offers lots of water recreation, including the Thunder Bay Wave Pool, Dare Devil Drop, Runaway Raft Ride, Inner Tubes on the Lazee River, Sunken ship and plank walk at Shipwreck Cove, Raging Rapids, Pirate's Plunge, a Skycoaster, and Splash Island for kids under 54" tall (with a kiddie-sized wave pool, a volcano with two slides, double tube slides and interactive water play elements). Just an hour or so drive from the Triangle.

LAST FRIDAYS   Hillsborough

201 N. Church St.
Hillsborough, NC 27278
(919) 643-2500 | www.hillsboroughartscouncil.org
One of the longest running and successful arts events in the Triangle, held April-September, on the lawn and spilling out onto the streets in front of the Old Courthouse downtown. Bands playing, arts and craft vendors, children's art events, and the ever-popular pie-eating contest. A little slice of Americana.

NC AQUARIUM AT FORT FISHER   Kure Beach

900 Loggerhead Rd.
Kure Beach, NC 28449
(866) 301- 3476 | www.ncaquariums.com
Watch the sea horses and pet the starfish. Interact with scuba divers who answer questions from the audience while swimming around with sharks, fish, skates, and other sea life! Located on US 421 about 15 miles south of Wilmington, just beyond Kure Beach. From Southport take the Southport-Fort Fisher Ferry.

CAROLINA TIGER RESCUE   Pittsboro

1940 Hanks Chapel Rd.
Pittsboro, NC 27312
(919) 542-4684 | www.cptigers.org
Formerly the Carnivore Preservation Trust, the nonprofit animal sanctuary offers guided tours by reservation only on Saturdays and Sundays at 10 am and 1 pm. The tours are guided by a trained docent and include tigers, leopards, jaguars, ocelots, and other exotic carnivore species. These educational tours allow you to view the animals up close (as close as five feet), and last approximately an hour and a half to two hours.

ACRO ENTERTAINMENT   Raleigh

Raleigh, NC
www.acroentertainment.com
Funky hula hooping, fire-breathing, juggling acrobatic street performers who usually show up at downtown festivals and events. Go to their website to find out where they'll be performing next.

ANNUAL GEM AND
MINERAL FESTIVAL
Raleigh

1025 Blue Ridge Rd.
Kerr Scott bldg at the State Fairgrounds
Raleigh, NC 27607
(919) 821-7400
Exhibitors present a wide variety of minerals, gems, crystals, beads and jewelry.

BUGFEST
Raleigh

Raleigh, NC
www.bugfest.org
Annual event presented by NC Museum of Natural Science, which houses some of the events. Also spills out into the streets around the museum and State Capitol. Best part of Bugfest is sampling the delectable creepy crawly dishes. Chocolate covered mill worms are tolerable. Be warned: Dad will have to try them first!

CAROLINA ROLLERGIRLS
Raleigh

Dalton Arena @ NC Fairgrounds
1025 Blue Ridge Rd.
Raleigh, NC 27607
www.carolinarollergirls.com
Fierce competition, rock-n-roll attitude, free-wheeling spirit... visit their website for home schedule.

FIRST FRIDAY
Raleigh

Raleigh, NC
www.godowntownraleigh.com/FirstFriday
One of Raleigh's most popular on-going events. Join the masses on a free, self-guided tour of local art galleries, restaurants, musical acts and alternative art venues each first Friday of the month. Usually cranks up around 6 and lasts way past bedtime. Artspace (201 E. Davie St.) is often the epicenter of activity and as good a place as any to start off.

GREEK FESTIVAL
Raleigh

Expo Center at the State Fairgrounds
Raleigh, NC 27607
(919) 781-4568 | www.holytrinityraleigh.org/greekfestival
Three-day event, annually held in September at the Expo Center. Food, music, dancing... Baklava, galaktoboureko or finikia anyone?

SATURDAY SCIENCE CINEMA AT THE NC MUSEUM OF NATURAL SCIENCES
Raleigh

11 W. Jones St.
Raleigh, NC 277601
(919) 733-7450 | www.naturalsciences.org/cinemaniac
Free movies and high-def wildlife adventures, every Saturday at 3 PM for you and your nature-loving film buff.

MCKEE'S CEDAR CREEK FARM
Rougemont

5011 Kiger Rd.
Rougemont, NC 27572
(919) 372-8065 | www.mckeemaze.com
12 acre adventurous maze, two acre interactive children's maze, haunted trail and corn field maze. Farm products for sale: pumpkins, gourds, corn stalks, mums, straw bales and bagged corn for wildlife feed. Mckee's is about 15 miles north of Durham in northern Orange County.

WRIGHTSVILLE BEACH
Rougemont

The quickest, easiest beach to access for an impromptu day trip to the beach. Takes about 2 hours from Raleigh, straight down I-40. We get an early start, play hard at the beach all day and then two exhausted girls sleep all the way home.

THE BEST DAD/CHILD
SPORTING EVENTS

CAROLINA RAILHAWKS
Cary

WakeMed Soccer Park
101 Soccer Park Dr.
Cary, NC 27511
(919) 859-2332 | www.carolinarailhawks.com

NASL professional soccer team based in Cary. On game day, the Rail-Hawks enter the field through a human tunnel made of kids. Kids gather at the northwest corner of the stadium 30 minutes before kickoff.

UNC TAR HEELS
Chapel Hill

Kenan Field House
Chapel Hill, NC 27514
www.tarheelblue.com

From Mia Hamm, perhaps the most popular women's soccer player in the world, to Michael Jordan, arguably the greatest player to ever dribble a basketball, UNC has certainly had its share of superstars traipsing along Franklin St. through the years. Kenan Stadium is one of the more picturesque settings for football on a cool, crisp Autumn afternoon and a great way to spend a Saturday with your little football fans. Come winter, the 22,000-seat Dean Dome is the place to be. Both UNC's men's and women's soccer teams are always awesome and fun to watch.

The Tar Heels compete in basketball, baseball, softball, football, lacrosse, tennis, field Hockey, volleyball, gymnastics, soccer, wresting, track and field, fencing, golf, and cross country.

DUKE UNIVERSITY BLUE DEVILS
Durham

118 Cameron Indoor Stadium
Durham, NC 27708
www.goduke.com

Duke University fields a number of championship-level teams in both men's and women's sports each year. Cheer on the football Blue Devils at historic Wallace Wade Stadium, site of the only Rose Bowl not played in California. The men's basketball team is a perennial powerhouse and 2010 national champs. The women's tennis team won the 2009 national championship. The lacrosse teams are always among the top-ranked teams in the nation.

The Blue Devils compete in basketball, baseball, softball, football, lacrosse, tennis, field Hockey, volleyball, gymnastics, soccer, wresting, track and field, fencing, golf, cross country and rowing.

SPORTING EVENTS

DURHAM BULLS

Durham

409 Blackwell St.
Durham, NC 27701
(919) 956-BULL | www.durhambulls.com

Team made famous by the movie Bull Durham, this is AAA minor league baseball at its best; fireworks after many home games and other fun kid activities such as running the bases with Wool-E-Bull.... Spongebob and Dora usually make appearances throughout the season. Stadium is adjacent to the American Tobacco Historic District which offers many places to eat and shop before and after the game.

NC CENTRAL EAGLES

Durham

1801 Fayetteville St.
Durham, NC 27707
www.nceaglepride.com

NCCU sponsors fourteen men's and women's sports teams that participate in NCAA Division I as a newly readmitted member of the Mid-Eastern Athletic Conference. Athletic teams include football, softball, baseball, basketball, track and field, tennis, volleyball, bowling, and golf. Most fun to catch a game with one of the Eagles big rivals, NC A&T or Winston-Salem State.

CAROLINA HURRICANES

Raleigh

RBC Center
1400 Edwards Mill Rd
Raleigh, NC 27607
(919) 467-7852 | www.carolinahurricanes.com

The 2006 NHL Stanley Cup Champs, Hurricane games are rowdy, raucous and a ton of fun! Request a shout out on the Jumbotron or have Stormy visit your seat for a special birthday surprise.

NC STATE WOLFPACK

Raleigh

Athletic Dept.
Weisiger Brown Building
2500 Warren Carroll Dr.
Raleigh, NC 27695
www.gopack.com

The Wolfpack field many competitive teams and, along with rivals UNC and Duke, are one of three Atlantic Coast Conference teams from the Triangle. NC State plays their football games at Carter-Finley Stadium and basketball games at the RBC Center, both of which are near the State Fairgrounds, which makes a perfect tail-gaiting spot!

The Wolfpack compete in basketball, baseball, softball, football, lacrosse, tennis, field Hockey, volleyball, gymnastics, soccer, wresting, track and field, fencing, golf, and cross country.

SHAW UNIVERSITY BEARS
Raleigh

118 E. South St.
Raleigh, NC 27601
www.shawbears.com
Follow the Garnet and White clad Bears and Lady Bears as they compete in NCAA Division II's CIAA conference in football, softball, baseball, basketball, track and field, tennis, volleyball, bowling, and golf.

ST. AUGUSTINE
UNIVERSITY FALCONS
Raleigh

1315 Oakwood Ave.
Raleigh, NC 27610
www.st-aug.edu/sports-page
The Falcons are a track and field powerhouse, winning 24 Division II titles during the George "Pup" Williams coaching tenure, beginning in 1976. The CIAA conference members also field teams in football, softball, baseball, basketball, tennis, volleyball, bowling, and golf.

102

ABOUT THE AUTHOR

Stephen Raburn is a writer and child advocate and, most importantly, WonderDad to Xia and Anika. He lives in Durham.

Stephen dedicates this book to his fellow dads across the Triangle who try their best to come up with a brilliant answer to the question: "Dad, what are we doing today?" and to his two amazing little girls with whom every second he gets to spend is a pleasure, honor and privilege.

LaVergne, TN USA
11 April 2011
223702LV00001B/53/P